THE MINIATURE PALMS
OF JAPAN

THE  MIN

TURE
PALMS OF JAPAN

Cultivating Kannonchiku and Shurochiku

by Yoshihiro Okita

and J. Leland Hollenberg

New York • WEATHERHILL • *Tokyo*

First edition, 1981

Published by John Weatherhill, Inc., of New York and Tokyo, with editorial offices at 7-6-13 Roppongi, Minato-ku, Tokyo 106, Japan. Protected by copyright under terms of the International Copyright Union; all rights reserved. Printed in the Republic of Korea and first published in Japan.

Library of Congress Cataloging in Publication Data: Okita, Yoshihiro. / The miniature palms of Japan. / Includes index. / 1. Rhapis excelsa. 2. Rhapis humilis. / 3. Miniature plants. I. Hollenberg, J. Leland, joint author. II. Title. / SB413. R44037 635.9'7745 81-387 / ISBN 0-8348-0160-4 AACRI

Contents

*Color plates appear between pages 22
and 23 and pages 38 and 39.*

Preface

The art of bonsai is well known in many parts of the world, including the United States, but the ancient art of growing dwarf *Rhapis* palms is little known outside Japan. Kannonchiku and shurochiku, as the two common *Rhapis* species are called, have become so thoroughly ingrained in the Japanese culture that most people think of them as indigenous to Japan. As the reader will see, this is not the case.

There are certain marked similarities between bonsai and these small palms. For example, the use of very small pots, techniques of root pruning, and soils low in nutrients are common features. However, there are also marked differences, many of which favor the palms. Unlike bonsai, these miniature palms are so adaptable that they can be grown indoors exclusively, if desired. As a result, their beauty can be enjoyed at all seasons of the year. Their constant renewal, by growing additional shoots, assures the owner a plant that will last a lifetime, with the attractive bonus of extra plants to enjoy, trade, or sell.

Until publication of this book, information on the art of kannonchiku and shurochiku has been quite scarce outside of Japan. To my knowledge, previous references are limited to articles in *Pacific Coast Nurseryman*, *Pacific Horticulture*, and *Principes*, the journal of the Palm Society.

There are three books in Japanese on kannonchiku and shurochiku. Two are introductory volumes, and the third is specialized information for commercial growers or advanced hobbyists. The present book is a translation and adaptation of one of the introductory works. The translation of this book into English has been a slow, but very rewarding, process.

The reader should be aware that I speak and read not a word of Japanese. I have been utterly dependent on translators and interpreters for the information contained in this book. My role has been one of an editor, rather than an author, although in some instances I have included a few sentences to convey my own experience with these plants.

Shortly after World War II, a society of *Rhapis* palm enthusiasts, known as the Kansokai, was formed in Japan. Its present director, Mr. Koichi Inoue, was instrumental in stimulating my interest in kannonchiku and shurochiku. He is a commercial grower, and twice he has visited me in the United States, bringing me many interesting *Rhapis* varieties and copies of books on their culture. His demonstrations of planting techniques and explanations of cultural principles have been extremely valuable. He has generously offered to consult with me on any problems or questions related to growing these palms, and I have made repeated use of his offer.

It is a pleasure to acknowledge the help of Mr. Inoue in making this book possible. When he learned that I was interested in producing an English translation of it, he offered to discuss the project with the author, Mr. Yoshihiro Okita. Through Mr. Inoue's influence, not only was permission obtained for translating the work into English, but Mr. Okita enthusiastically set about writing descriptions about and photographing the newest varieties that had appeared since his book was originally published in Japan in 1972.

Mr. Robert Fisher of the art department at the University of Redlands, while a visiting scholar in Japan, was instrumental in arranging contacts for me with Mr. Inoue.

This project could not have succeeded without the generous help given me by Dr. Yasuyuki Owada, professor of sociology at the University of Redlands. He has translated for me all of the letters that were written in Japanese. He located people, most of them students, who were willing to work on the translation, and he also helped on points that seemed ambiguous.

The following people served as translators: Keiko Nakao (who did the largest portion), Dr. Noriharu Umetsu, Kuniko Ninomiya,

Yukiko Sakamoto, Madoka Kawasaki, Genshi Shigekawa, Yoshi-hiko Nakamichi, and Robert Gano.

I am grateful for the skilled editing and many helpful suggestions given by Ruth P. Stevens of John Weatherhill, Inc. She has provided the organizational framework and guided the format of the book.

Finally, my wife, Anna, and my son, Jim, were generous with help in typing and retyping the manuscript. Anna's editorial efforts were also very useful, and her encouragement and patience kept me going.

It is hoped that this book on kannonchiku and shurochiku will produce considerable interest in these remarkable palms, for they deserve to be much more widely grown and appreciated throughout the world.

J. LELAND HOLLENBERG

THE MINIATURE PALMS
OF JAPAN

Introduction

Kannonchiku (*Rhapis excelsa*) and shurochiku (*Rhapis humilis*) are referred to jointly as kansochiku. In recent years, kansochiku have become very popular in Japan, and many people are raising them. What accounts for the growing attraction of these miniature palms? First of all, they are very beautiful and a pleasure to have around. Secondly, they are easy to grow, and the growing process can be an absorbing pastime. The reasons for the increase in popularity are numerous, but foremost is the esthetic value of these beautiful and graceful plants.

Great variety is found in kansochiku, for there are over a hundred named cultivars. About fifty of these are striped (*shimafu*) or spotted (*zufu*) varieties, and fifty are solid green (*aoba*) varieties. The leaves may be large or small and have various shapes, depending on the variety. Some cultivars have leaves that are very shiny, and the variegated plants with their stripes or spots have different leaf patterns. Because of the attractive shapes and colors, the plants fit very well in both Japanese and Western homes, and they add a feeling of calm and grace to the surroundings.

People who raise kansochiku plants never tire of them. The plants bring a special charm into their daily lives. Moreover, kansochiku are evergreen plants and can be enjoyed all year round. One of the good points of these plants is that they are green and attractive even during the winter months. Another good feature is that they are very sturdy and easy to grow. Unlike bonsai, which must be kept outside almost exclusively, kansochiku can, if desired, be kept indoors most of the time.

3

Originally these plants came from the southern regions of Asia, so people thought that a special growing environment was required; however, this is not so. Because kansochiku are from the south, they are more sensitive to cold than many Japanese plants; but they in fact have more resistance to cold than most people realize, particularly if the exposure to cold is gradual. Under these circumstances, most kansochiku plants will eventually be able to stand even freezing temperatures without dying.

These palms can be trained to withstand cold, but care must be taken so that no snow or frost touches the leaves, and the roots must not be allowed to freeze. On cold nights, if the number of potted plants is few, it is best to put them inside. If there are many plants, they can be placed by a sunny window, or a makeshift hothouse can be constructed out of plastic sheet material. If shurochiku are planted outside in the ground, it is best to put them on the southern side of the building, and if the night gets very cold or if it looks like a frost is approaching, then plastic can be draped over the plants. With simple precautions such as these, the plants will be able to survive most winters.

Kansochiku have several good points when compared to other plants. First of all, they are very resistant to insects and disease. Another advantage is that they resist pollution, dust, and smoke, which many plants cannot tolerate. Another point in their favor is that daily care is very simple, and once the plants have been given a proper place in the house or outside, the rest is simply a matter of daily watering and periodic use of insecticide and fertilizer. By use of a coarse-textured potting mix, such as one designed for African violets, watering can be reduced in frequency to about once a week. All of these features make kansochiku very practical plants for modern living.

While many plants such as bonsai take a great deal of skill, kansochiku have simple cultural requirements, and even a beginner will soon have almost as much knowledge and skill as a veteran. These plants can be raised in a very limited space—for example, a veranda, a porch, or anywhere that can accommodate the pot. Unlike some plants, kansochiku do not need direct sunlight as long as they have an ample light supply of some kind, such as from a light bulb or daylight through a window.

The authors have experience with one plant that has been grow-

Kannonchiku and shurochiku.

ing for ten years with only the light of a forty-watt fluorescent bulb. Even though this plant is not as strong as some others, it still has green and shiny leaves, and every year it sends up shoots. This ability to adapt to less desirable conditions is not found in most other plants. Because of the many advantages, growing kansochiku is becoming one of the most rewarding new indoor plant activities and is attracting followers not only in Japan but in other parts of the world as well.

Another good feature is that kansochiku propagation is simple. Kansochiku are not grown from seeds, cuttings, or graftings. Instead, each year from one to three new shoots will come up from the potting mix surrounding the plant. When given water and other necessary care, these shoots will flourish and soon become additional plants.

A recent development is the propagation of kansochiku as a sideline business. This is proving to be very profitable to many people. Because it is very difficult to propagate these plants from seeds, and impossible to propagate them from cuttings or graftings, the price remains almost constant. Also, the demand for these plants tends to rise every year, which makes growing them attractive as a source of extra income. Large facilities are not needed, care and labor are minimal, and the risk of loss is low.

1

The Character of Kansochiku

Kansochiku plants are native to Southeast Asia and neighboring subtropical regions. Growing typically in the shade of trees in valleys in very humid areas, they are common in southern China, Taiwan, Laos, Malaysia, and Vietnam. They have also been found on Yakushima, a small island just south of the Japanese island of Kyushu.

The origin of the name kannonchiku is believed to date from around 1600, when the plants were first brought into Japan. From Southeast Asia to Japan is quite a long distance, and for this reason travelers carrying *Rhapis* palm plants stopped off at Okinawa, where there was a temple dedicated to Kannon, the Buddhist goddess of mercy. This temple became a regular stopping point and a place of rest for the traders of these palms, and thus it is not surprising that they gave the plants the name of the Kannon temple. The plants were also given, mistakenly, the name *chiku,* which means bamboo. They are in fact members of the palm family. In ancient times, according to *Yamato Honzo,* an early botanical book, these plants were called *hobichiku,* which means phoenix-tail bamboo, because the leaves were thought to resemble both bamboo and the tail of the mythical phoenix, called *ho-o* in Japanese.

Centuries ago, when these plants were first being imported, people did not differentiate between the kannonchiku and the shurochiku, but as time went on the realization grew that they were two distinctly different plant species. Thus *Rhapis excelsa* was given the

6

外斑竹　漳州府志云節間有斑文似湘妃戻膜所餘
者〇今按本邦處ヲニアリ

外鳳尾竹　俗呼觀音竹泉州府志出本邦ニモアリ葉ヒロク
竹小ナリ綱目ニ所謂鳳尾竹葉細三分與此異

外橙竹　橙竹ニ大小アリ大ニ二種アリ一種ハ葉短クツヨシ
小ニ〇不高一種ハ色淡黒葉大ニ莖高ク長レスヤレ是ヲ犬
橙橺竹ト云ワトモ又別ニ一種小橙竹アリ甚小也盆ニ
植テ可愛葉莖與大同〇本草曰一名實竹其莖似

ナトノ如ク一處ヨリ多生ス大アリ小アリ小ナル者モ長
シ又杖トスヘシ

外黄金碧

梭可為杖杖
甚裏ラオソル暖處ニ宜シ冬春八上
ニラ水ヒラスヘシ一處ニ叢生ス其莖杖ニシテ輕ク勁多
不折諸草木ノ内杖ニ用ルモノ多シ是ヲ尤シトス
竹帯ニ出タリ黄竹ニシテ青筋アリ雄竹ナリ又一
大名竹ニ似テ不同京都北野草木屋ニモアリ又一
種スチ竹ト云竹アリ女竹ノ類ナリ白キ冬ヲ筋アリ是
亦大名竹ト不同

雷丸　竹ノ精纂ヨリ生ス松ニ茯苓アルカ如シ土中ニ生ス
苗モ蔓葉モナシ猶クルク如クミ皮黒ク肉白シ皮甚力
タレ亦キハ毒アリ藥鉼ニ三テ大風子ヲ雷丸ト稱ス甚非

Yamato Honzo, *an early Japanese botanical text.*

name kannonchiku, and *Rhapis humilis* was named shurochiku. The latter name is taken from a plant called *shuro,* which is the Japanese name for the palm *Trachycarpus fortunei.* Thus shurochiku means literally "palmlike bamboo." However, the most obvious difference between shurochiku and bamboo is that the latter is hollow and shurochiku is not. Despite their names, kansochiku themselves are not members of the bamboo family but are monocotyledons and are actually palms.

CHARACTERISTICS OF KANSOCHIKU

STEM Both kannonchiku and shurochiku plants are fairly small evergreens. Characteristically, mature specimens never have any leaves or branches coming out of the side of the stem except near the very top. Rarely growing higher than three meters (about three yards) when grown in containers, their average height is from one to three meters, and their average stem diameter is about three centimeters (about one inch). Kannonchiku are usually smaller on the average than shurochiku. Kannonchiku plants reach a height of about two meters (six feet) when mature, while shurochiku plants are about five meters (fifteen feet) in maturity.

The trunks of both these plants have the growth rings associated with the bamboo plant, although they are actually palms. These rings are the marks left after the leaves fall. Usually the rings are not visible because of the hairlike "bark" that grows heavily on the stem. This hair is characteristic of most palms, and it serves to protect the stem and young leaves. The hair covering will stay on the trunk and not fall unless it is pulled off or unless the plant is very old and the hair begins to rot.

LEAVES The leaves, or fronds, are the most important part of the kansochiku because they are the plants' source of beauty. To many people these leaves resemble the palm of a hand. When the leaves grow, they never overlap but are always slightly offset so as to receive the greatest amount of sunlight. The leaves are oval-shaped with the outside end more pointed than the inside, and the veins run parallel to the stem of the leaf, as is the case with bamboo. The lengths of the leaves vary from about 10 to 40 centimeters (4–16

Shurochiku leaves.

Kannonchiku leaves.

Kansochiku stem.

inches) and the widths vary from 1.5 to 13 centimeters (0.6–5.0 inches). The leaves are usually dark green in color, and the tips have a sawtooth edge. The shurochiku plant usually has a narrower and longer leaf than the kannonchiku, and the leaf tends to droop downward, giving the plant a gentle appearance. The kannonchiku plant has a thick, broad leaf giving it a more robust appearance. There are about one hundred named cultivars of kansochiku, and each has somewhat different leaf characteristics.

Roots   Rather than having a single main root with many small root hairs extending from it, kansochiku have a system of numerous larger hairs and no main root. The color of these roots is white at first and then gradually turns yellow, until finally the color is brown by the time of death. The roots are strong and flexible, and even if parts are broken off, more will grow in their place. Transplanting and propagation are thus very easy, because when the young shoots are separated from the main plant, the damage to the roots will repair itself.

The ideal temperature for root growth is from about 15–30° C

Kannonchiku roots.

Flowers and seeds.

(60–87° F). This means that the best times to transplant or divide the plants are the spring and fall.

FLOWERS AND SEEDS   Kansochiku plants bloom between spring and summer, and their flowers resemble various types of coral in shape and color. Flowers sprout from the area between the base of the stem of the leaf and the hair of the trunk. The flowers are a very light yellow or pink, and, if pollinated, small berries will form as the flowers later dry and drop off. Kansochiku have what are termed male and female plants. To be fertilized, the female plants must be pollinated, either by insects or with human assistance. There are considerably fewer female plants, so people who are lucky enough to have berries form should let them ripen. If they are planted and kept moist and warm, sometimes new plants will actually grow from these seeds. Germination usually occurs in 45 to 120 days.

Because of the scarcity of the female plants, it is very difficult to raise kansochiku from seeds. And even though there may be berries on a plant, there will not necessarily be a great number of seeds. It takes so much time, energy, and equipment to raise the plants from seeds that it is not a very practical or productive method. In Japan, propagation is achieved almost exclusively by removing the young shoots formed by the parent and replanting them in individual pots.

2

History of Kansochiku in Japan

Kansochiku plants were introduced to Japan around the year 1600, and for a long time they have been loved by the Japanese people and are now firmly ingrained in their culture. Most people think that shurochiku were introduced first, but it is more probable that both kinds of plants were imported at about the same time and that they were not identified as separate species until later. The time of the variegated (striped and spotted) kansochiku's arrival in Japan is also ambiguous, but most people think they appeared during the early part of the nineteenth century.

In the first period after their introduction into Japan (from about 1600 to 1925), kannonchiku plants were grown by different methods from those now in use. At present it is popular to grow them in pots, but they were originally raised in outdoor gardens. Because of their susceptibility to cold, they could be grown only in the warmer regions of Japan, where they gave the gardens a tropical feeling and quickly became very popular.

In this first period, shurochiku plants were more popular than kannonchiku plants. This was mainly because they grew faster, were larger, and could better withstand cold. A new type of kannonchiku, the striped plant, probably originated during this time. This event was first recorded around 1700, but the new type did not become popular until much later because they were difficult to grow well. The knowledge and equipment of the times were limited, and when the plants grew, their stripes were not uniform or were in some other way imperfect. As a result, it took a long time for the popularity of this type of plant to rise to its present level.

The second period was roughly from 1925 to 1945. In this period the main development was the increasing popularity of the striped kannonchiku plants. From about 1920 to 1930 many similar variegated plants became popular, and from them were developed many of the striped kannonchiku varieties we are familiar with now. People began buying, trading, and growing them to such an extent that soon the balance between the supply and demand was lost, and the prices shot to exorbitant levels. For example, in 1928 a certain striped kannonchiku with five to six leaves of moderate size cost the equivalent of about $15 in Japan. By 1935 this same plant was priced at $230 to $270, and in 1938 records show that one plant was sold for as much as $3000.

Kannonchiku plants were more popular than shurochiku after about 1935. As a result, many more plants were imported from Taiwan and other places of native origin, and eventually many new varieties of these plants, both variegated and all green, were discovered. As interest in these plants on a national scale increased, there sprang up various activities like swap meets, at which people would trade plants from different areas, or kannonchiku clubs, where members could share their experiences and enthusiasm.

Many new cultivars or varieties were discovered during the years 1925–40. In order to keep everything in Japan uniform for propagation and distribution purposes, a list was issued that named and described all the varieties of kannonchiku, and this list was revised and circulated yearly. The first list was published in 1940, and it contained thirty-five varieties. When World War II began, the swap meets and interest groups were forced to discontinue their activities, and people growing kansochiku declined in number until after the war.

The third period covers the years from about 1945 to 1960. After the war ended, the popularity of kansochiku plants increased again, and in 1947 the Japan Kansochiku Association, or Kansokai, was officially organized. This association's most important achievement was that it standardized nationwide the formerly unofficial list of kannonchiku varieties. Prior to the formation of the Kansokai, each area or region of the country had its own list, and many of the names were duplicated. Through the efforts of the Kansokai, each variety was given its own official name. In 1947 the official list had fifty varieties. The swap meets, interest groups, and other activities

Kansochiku annual ranking list (1972).

began to increase again, and in 1949 the first exhibition of kannon-chiku was held in Izu, to the southwest of Tokyo. This event resulted in more interest in exhibitions, which were soon held in other places. During this period the most popular plants were the following kansochiku: Kinshi, Kannonchikushima, Hinodenishiki, Kinsho, Asahinishiki, Toryumon, Hakkokinshi, Zuikonishiki, and Taiheiden.

The fourth period in kansochiku development dates from about 1960 to the present. In this period, a second boom of interest in kansochiku occurred, resulting in part from the discovery of the Tenzannoshima plant. The most popular plants in this period have been Tenzannoshima, Darumanoshima, Kotobuki, Tokainishiki, Zuikonishiki, Hinodenishiki, Kannonchikushima, Taiheiden, Heiwaden, Mangetsu, Aikokuden, Shippoden, Tenzan, Koban, and Keigetsu.

As had happened previously, the boom led to an imbalance between supply and demand, causing prices to rise sharply. Later these very high prices plummeted, mainly because the most popular plant for a time became a solid variety, which multiplies faster than the variegated plants. Because the number of propagators was increasing and the conditions and methods were improving, the supply gradually caught up with and surpassed the demand. Another cause of the price drop was that many people were raising the plants for profit and were not especially interested in the plants themselves. Thus when they saw that the market was dropping, they completely ceased raising them. With these factors combined, the prices gradually leveled off.

Kansochiku prices eventually stabilized, and popularity shifted from the solid varieties back to the striped. The principal reason was that even though the variegated types do not multiply as quickly as the solid ones, they have far more variety and are more beautiful. After prices leveled off, it again became possible for ordinary people to buy the plants, which became popular as gifts or as household plants once more.

At present there are about one hundred varieties, and about fifty of these are variegated. In the future, this number will probably increase. At present, the propagators and admirers of kansochiku in Japan are located mostly in the regions to the south of and including Tokyo. The reason the plants are not as numerous farther north is that a cold climate is not as favorable as the warmer regions. However, with improved technology it looks very possible that, in the future, growing activity will become more prevalent farther north as well.

3

Genealogical Groups

Today there are over one hundred varieties of kansochiku (kannonchiku and shurochiku), and new cultivars are still being discovered or developed. Kannonchiku and shurochiku are, of course, the two main lineages, and each of them can be divided into three groups according to leaf pattern—solid green, striped, and spotted.

GENEALOGICAL GROUPS OF KANNONCHIKU   Kannonchiku are divided into four groups depending on their places of origin.

Native Group   These varieties were introduced into Japan during the very early days, and they have been under cultivation for a long time. The leaves tend to split into segments, and their stripes are relatively narrow.

Rakanchiku Group   Plants in this group came from the southern part of China (the Canton region). The leaves are narrow and split readily into segments. They resemble the shurochiku species to some extent.

Imported Group   This group of kannonchiku was imported from places other than Taiwan and southern China. Therefore, their characteristics depend on the various places of origin.

Taiwanchiku Group   These varieties were brought to Japan from Taiwan in considerable numbers just before World War II. The leaves are large and wide and do not split easily. The stripes are wide, and the stems are very thick.

GENEALOGICAL GROUPS OF SHUROCHIKU   It is often thought of shurochiku that there are two main genealogical groups, large and small. This is incorrect, for these size variations are often due to different environmental conditions. For example, plants may have small leaves when they are grown in small pots, when the soil is poor, or when more water is needed. Under the opposite conditions, when they are planted outside in the ground, the leaves may be large and wide.

Careful study shows that all shurochiku plants, including such named varieties as Shurochikushima, Kinsho, and Kimboshi, have a common lineage.

Genealogical Tree of Kannonchiku

I. NATIVE GROUP

Solid Green
Kannonchiku ── Kannonchikushima ──── Hakuhonishiki
            ├─ Kinshi ─────────┬── Zuikonishiki
            │   └── Chiyodazuru
            ├─ Akatsuki
            ├─ Ogonmaru
            ├─ Nikkoden
            ├─ Uchuden
            ├─ Hakutsurunishiki
            └─ Ayanishiki

Fukuju ──────┬─ Kotobuki
             ├─ Hakuju
             ├─ Choju
             └─ Fukujunishiki

2. RAKANCHIKU GROUP

Toryumon
Hakkonohikari

3. IMPORTED GROUP

Otohime
Himedaruma
Ho-o
Shoryu
Daimyo
Meisei

4. TAIWANCHIKU GROUP

Daruma ──────┬─ Darumanoshima
             ├─ Shozannishiki
             └─ Darumanozu

Tenzan ──────┬─ Tenzannoshima
             ├─ Tenzanshiroshima
             ├─ Tenshi
             └─ Showanishiki

Daikokuten ──┬─ Daikokutennoshima
             └─ Daikokunishiki

Mangetsu ────┬─ Mangetsunoshima
             └─ Mangetsunozu

Kodaruma ────┬─ Kodarumanishiki
             ├─ Kodarumanoshima
             ├─ Zuishonishiki
             └─ Koganenishiki

Koban ─────── Kobannishiki
Heiwaden ──── Towaden
Hakkokinshi ─┬─ Kinkonishiki
             └─ Shirotaenishiki
Shiho ─────── Shihonoshima
Keigetsu ──── Keigetsunoshima

Shippoden ─────────── Shippodennoshima
Aikokuden ─────────── Aikokudennoshima

Tokainishiki
Nanzannishiki
Eizannishiki
Taiheiden
Hinodenishiki
Daifukuden
Choyo
Fukiden
Gyokuho
Gyokuryu

Genealogical Tree of Shurochiku

Shurochikuao ──────┬─ Shurochikushima
                   ├─ Hakuseiden
                   ├─ Kinsho
                   ├─ Kinboshi
                   └─ Hakumeijo

18 GENEALOGICAL GROUPS

4

Varieties of Kansochiku

STRIPED KANNONCHIKU PLANTS

AIKOKUDENNOSHIMA (Hall of Patriotism Stripes). As its name implies, this variety came from the plant Aikokuden. Registered in 1979, its big leaves have clear yellowish-white stripes. The green background color has a blackish hue. The leaf surface is frosted in appearance, rather than shiny.

The wide, thick leaves have a magnificent shape. From the middle to the tip, each leaf droops gracefully. At the present time, this variety is still quite scarce.

AKATSUKI (Dawn). *See Color Plate 22.* Akatsuki is a kannonchiku variety that developed spontaneously as a sport of one of the plants native to Taiwan. It was very popular in the period after World War II when the interest in kansochiku grew again, and it remains one of the more popular stripe-patterned kinds of kannonchiku.

When the leaf starts to come out, the stripes have a pale milky color, after which the white gradually becomes dominant, and then the green color spreads from the tip to the whole leaf. It is characteristic of this variety to show this delicate transformation in leaf pattern, a change very similar to that in Hinodenishiki, which also belongs to the taiwanchiku group. However, Akatsuki developed first, and it has a small and thin leaf, a short leafstalk, and a slim trunk. It is thus easy to tell the difference between the two kinds of kannonchiku.

Akatsuki is very strong and easy to grow, but a nicely striped

19

specimen is hard to cultivate. This variety has a long history and is a suitable plant for beginners.

ASAHINISHIKI (Rising Sun Brocade). Asahinishiki was discovered among the new shoots from some variegated kansochiku plants that were imported from Taiwan during World War II. It was registered in 1951.

The process of the change in the leaf and stripe colors resembles that of Akatsuki. The stripe has a pale milky color when the leaf starts to come out. This color then gradually disappears. Later the green color spreads inwards from the tip of the leaf. Finally all parts of the leaf become yellow-green in color. Rather than being sharply defined, the hues in this striped variety of kannonchiku are rather diffuse.

Asahinishiki is very strong and, growing quickly, easy to cultivate. The leaf is wide and thick, giving it an image of stiffness. Since its price is relatively low, it is one of the most suitable plants for beginners among the striped varieties of kannonchiku plants.

AYANISHIKI (Figured Brocade). *See Color Plate 25.* Ayanishiki was developed from Zuikonishiki and registered in 1976. The whitish color of its stripes is similar to that of Zuikonishiki. However, while Zuikonishiki's stripes, which are both narrow and wide, seem to have been painted on with a brush, Ayanishiki's stripes look as though they have been sprayed on all over the leaf. Most of the stripes are even narrower than those of Zuikonishiki, but here and there some wide stripes do appear.

Ayanishiki produces a high percentage of new shoots with good variegation. Moreover, the rate of production of new shoots is very high. Thus, even though this is a recent introduction, it is rapidly becoming available and popular.

CHIYODAZURU (Chiyoda Crane). *See Color Plate 21.* Chiyodazuru was derived from Kinshi, which is a variegated form of a native-group kannonchiku plant. This is a relatively new variety, having been registered in 1966.

In this variety the stripe pattern remains well defined throughout, whereas in the case of its ancestor Kinshi the stripe pattern is clear when the leaf starts to come out and then gradually becomes obscured.

Chiyodazuru is very strong and easy to cultivate, and it readily grows new shoots. Irregularity of the stripe pattern is not observed at all. Chiyodazuru has a strong capacity to multiply. Today, it has become very popular, spawning its own fan clubs.

CHOJU (Long Happiness). Choju is a variegated form of Fukuju, which is one of the native-group plants. Choju was registered in 1971 and thus is one of the more recent varieties.

The stripe pattern develops as follows: when the leaf first emerges, milk-white stripes appear. Then the color gradually turns to green, starting from the tip of the leaf, and eventually the pattern becomes less clear. These changes contrast sharply with Kotobuki, which was also derived from Fukuju.

The handsome leaf droops, and its tip is curled gently inward, giving this variety a graceful and dignified appearance.

The plant is very strong and easy to grow, and it readily develops new shoots. There is seldom any irregularity in the stripe pattern.

DAIKOKUNISHIKI (Fortune Brocade). *See Color Plate 3.* This variety comes from Daikokuten and was registered in 1973. It has beautiful yellow stripes on its deep green leaves, much like Daikoku-tennoshima, which also comes from Daikokuten. Unlike Daiko-kutennoshima, however, this variety does not show its stripes clearly when the newest leaves open. The faint stripes, which are greenish yellow at first, gradually become lighter and more distinct.

The trunk is short, giving the plant a rather dwarfed appearance. The leaves are very thick and heavy.

Daikokunishiki is a valuable plant and in great demand. The plant is quite strong and easy to multiply, but, as with numerous other striped kansochiku, new shoots having a good stripe pattern are not common. As a result, the plant is quite scarce.

DAIKOKUTENNOSHIMA (Fortune Stripes). Daikokutennoshima was derived from a popular variety, Daikokuten, which belongs to the taiwanchiku group. This unusual variety was discovered only recently and was registered in 1972.

The stripe pattern consists of beautiful clear yellow stripes appearing on a deep green background. The attractive leaves are thick and large, and the plant has high ornamental value. As with Tenzannoshima, Nanzannishiki, and Mangetsunoshima, growers are expecting wide future propagation of Daikokutennoshima. However, as is common among striped kannonchiku plants, the pattern of this variety tends to become irregular, and the number of plants will probably not increase rapidly.

DARUMANOSHIMA (Dharma's Stripes). *See Color Plate 4.* Darumanoshima was derived from Daruma, which is a member of the taiwanchiku group. It was registered in 1960. This is the most popular variety among high-quality striped cultivars.

Clear, beautiful yellow stripes appear on a deep green background. The appearance of the leaf is especially attractive. Very glossy and thick, it droops gracefully. The leafstalks are thick and short, and the vertical distance between them is small. Therefore, this is a rather diminutive variety. The tendency to develop an irregular stripe pattern is relatively low, and the plant is very strong and easy to grow. As a result, there are many people who are fond of this variety.

EIZANNISHIKI (Prosperous Mountain Brocade). *See Color Plate 16.* This variety originated in Taiwan, where growers plant many seeds and offer the most promising new shoots, especially variegated ones, for sale. Such was the case with Eizannishiki. This plant had never been divided before it was purchased and brought to Japan. It was registered in 1973 and has held the highest position in each Ranking Table since that time. In 1975 a single choice division sold for nearly $10,000.

The trunk of Eizannishiki is short, making the plant compact. Each frond tends to separate into several rather narrow leaflets, giving the plant a delicate, graceful appearance. Very beautiful clear yellowish-white stripes typically appear all over each leaf. The stripe pattern is unique, reminding one of the strokes of a brush.

Eizannishiki is not difficult to grow if overly strong light is avoided. Its root system is rather weak and does not tolerate heavy applications of fertilizer. Because it has a high percentage of nicely patterned new shoots, it is relatively easy to multiply. At present there is more demand for this remarkable plant than any other variety.

FUKUJUNISHIKI (Lucky Felicitations Brocade). Fukujunishiki was

1. Tenzanshiroshima

2. Tenzannoshima

3. Daikokunishiki

4. Darumanoshima

5. Kobannishiki

6. Zuishonishiki

7. Kodarumanishiki

8. Kinkonishiki

9. Shirotaenishiki

10. Tenmanishiki

11. Toyonishiki

12. Hinodenishiki

13. Hakkonohikari

14. Tokainishiki

15. Nanzannishiki

16. Eizannishiki

derived from Fukuju and was registered in 1980. It has slim white stripes on the entire surface of the leaf. The leaf surface is smooth and shiny. The medium-sized leaf droops inward at the tip. This is an elegant and dainty variety.

Kotobuki, which is also derived from Fukuju, has a low rate of production of good plants because the stripe pattern tends to become irregular. In contrast, Fukujunishiki has a very stable stripe pattern and a high percentage of good new shoots. Because of its rapid multiplication, it is likely to become very widespread.

HAKKOKINSHI (White Ray Brocade Thread). Hakkokinshi was introduced after World War II and belongs to the taiwanchiku group. It became widely known during the renewal of interest in kansochiku after World War II and has become very popular.

White, very fine stripes appear all over the leaf. The stripe pattern is a little unclear, and in some plants stripes are almost entirely lacking. The leaf is large and thick, and the leafstalk is thick and short.

The plant is very strong and easy to grow and thus has very high multiplication ability. Hakkokinshi is a suitable plant of the striped type of kannonchiku for beginners.

From this variety two cultivars were derived, Shirotacnishiki, which has pure white, clear wide stripes, and Kinkonishiki, which has yellow-white stripes. Both are popular varieties.

HAKKONOHIKARI (Boundless Light). *See Color Plate 13.* Hakkonohikari belongs to the rakanchiku group. It has long been a popular variety, but recently the number of specimens has decreased.

The leaf has a strong tendency to split. The plant has a narrow leaf that, rather than drooping, actually points slightly upward. Very rarely do all the leaves have stripe patterns, and the pattern varies from leaf to leaf. Sometimes several stripes appear on only one side of the leaf, or a large stripe can appear in the leaf's center.

The plant is quite vigorous and grows readily. The multiplication ability is very high, since it easily produces new shoots.

HAKUHONISHIKI (White Phoenix Brocade). *See Color Plate 19.* Hakuhonishiki belongs to the native group and was derived from Kannonchikushima. It was registered in 1963.

The stripe pattern is very similar to that of Kannonchikushima, so people sometimes confuse the two varieties. In Hakuhonishiki the white color is prominent, as indicated in its name (*haku* means white in Japanese). When its leaf first opens, the stripe pattern is quite clear.

The plant is very strong and easy to grow. However, a leaf that has considerable white area is easily burned by strong light. The stripe pattern often becomes irregular, so well-patterned plants are rare and in great demand.

HAKUJU (White Felicitations). *See Color Plate 26.* Hakuju originated from Fukuju, which was derived from one of the native-group plants. It was registered in 1959. The stripe pattern is close to pure white, while Kotobuki, which also originated from Fukuju, has yellow stripes. When a new leaf first opens, the stripes have a slight yellowish color, and they then gradually become closer to white.

The leaf is medium-sized, thin, and drooping. The tip of the leaf is curled gently inward. The plant is very strong and easy to grow if the stripe pattern is subdued. If the stripe pattern is vivid, more care should be taken because the leaf burns easily.

It is uncommon to see a Hakuju specimen, even though this variety was registered quite some time ago. Its scarcity is probably due to the fact that the stripes tend to become irregular, and therefore a perfectly patterned plant is very rare. Hakuju is now a highly prized variety.

HAKUTSURUNISHIKI (White Crane Brocade). *See Color Plate 24.* This was found as a sport of the all-green Namikannonchiku and was registered in 1976. Thus it derives from the native group of kansochiku. It has very slim, snow-white stripes spread over the surface of each leaf. In some respects it is similar to Zuikonishiki. The stripes of Hakutsurunishiki tend to be narrower and distributed more evenly on all the leaves.

The rate of producing new shoots is high, and most of the new shoots retain good variegation. Even though it is a recent introduction, this variety is becoming numerous and easy to acquire.

HINODENISHIKI (Sunrise Brocade). *See Color Plate 12.* Hinodenishiki belongs to the taiwanchiku group and was registered in 1942.

It has a long history for a striped kannonchiku plant and is very popular.

The leaf is large and thick. The leafstalk is thick and short. The trunk is thick, and the distance between leafstalks is short. Hinodenishiki has a pleasing stripe pattern. When the leaf starts to come out, milk-white stripes appear clearly on the green background, and then the stripes become yellowish. Finally the greenish color appears at the tip and extends to all parts of the leaf.

The plant is very strong. Although growth is a little slow, the plant is easy to cultivate and has a good ability to multiply.

KANNONCHIKUSHIMA (Striped Kannon Bamboo). Kannonchikushima is a cultivar that appeared as a variegation of one of the native-group plants. This variety has a very long history, and its presence was recognized in the middle Edo period (seventeenth century). It is the oldest known of all striped kannonchiku plants. Kannonchikushima played an important role in the development of kansochiku as a popular ornamental plant in Japan.

The stripes of Kannonchikushima have a yellowish color when the leaf starts to come out, and gradually the color changes to white. This variety has excellent ornamental value.

In spite of the long history of Kannonchikushima, the present number is still small. This is because the stripe pattern deteriorates in many new shoots, and the plant has a poor multiplication rate. However, the difficulty of obtaining good offspring is one of the plant's charms. This fact plus the beauty of the plant will no doubt maintain its popularity.

KEIGETSUNOSHIMA (Benevolent Moon Stripes). Registered in 1979, this plant came from Keigetsu and retains its parent's characteristically large, drooping leaves. It has brilliant yellowish-white stripes on the leaves, the surfaces of which have a soft appearance. There is remarkable similarity to Aikokudennoshima, which was also registered in 1979. Both have thick leaves, but Keigetsunoshima has a considerably more brilliant stripe pattern.

Care must be taken to avoid excessive light in order to prevent burning of the wider stripes. The retention of a good stripe pattern in new shoots is low, making nicely variegated Keigetsunoshima specimens scarce.

KINKONISHIKI (Golden Ray Brocade). *See Color Plate 8.* Kinkonishiki appeared among the offspring from Hakkonishiki, which belongs to the taiwanchiku group. This new variety was designated as Kinkonishiki and registered in 1963. It is a popular variety.

The leaf is big and thick, the leafstalk is thick and short, and the trunk is substantial. There are two stripe patterns in this variety. One has indistinct yellowish-green stripes in an early stage, and then the stripes gradually change to yellowish-white. The other also has yellowish-green stripes that are not sharply defined, but the stripes do not turn white, and the yellowish-green stripes become more distinct. (In contrast, the parent variety, Hakkonishiki, has wide yellowish-white stripes.)

Kinkonishiki is very strong and easy to grow. The stripe pattern is beautiful, giving the plant a high ornamental value. However, since the stripe pattern easily becomes disordered, it is very difficult to get choice plants. This challenge is one reason for Kinkonishiki's rising popularity.

KINSHI (Brocade Thread). Kinshi is a variety that appeared as a sport from one of the native-group plants, and it is steadily becoming more popular. This variety has a long history. Discovered in about 1935, it became very popular and high priced around the time of World War II. Now this variety is widely sought as one of the most desirable striped kannonchiku plants, and it is suitable for beginners.

The stripe pattern develops as follows: when the leaf starts to come out, clear, narrow white stripes appear all over the leaf; then the stripes gradually become darker.

The plant is quite strong and easy to grow. There is no irregularity in the stripe pattern, and it has a high ability to multiply. From Kinshi two new varieties were developed: Zuikonishiki and Chiyodazuru. Both of these varieties have become very popular with growers of kansochiku plants.

KOBANNISHIKI (Golden Coin Brocade). *See Color Plate 5.* Kobannishiki was derived from a popular variety, Koban, which belongs to the taiwanchiku group. It was registered in 1967.

Like Koban, this plant's leaf is medium-sized and thick, and it seldom splits. The leafstalk is thick and short. The vertical distance between leafstalks is short, and thus the plant is rather diminutive.

The unusual stripe pattern reveals delicate and subtle changes. When the leaf starts to come out, large portions of it show a milky white. Later the color turns greenish, with numerous fine white stripes appearing. If too much fertilizer is given, the white coloring may be temporarily obscured by green. Kobannishiki's outstanding leaf and stripe pattern give the plant a high ornamental value. To enhance its white blush appearance, use lower light, less nitrogen in the fertilizer, and lower temperature.

This strong plant easily produces new plants, and irregularity in the stripe pattern is rare. Therefore, the multiplication rate of this variety is high, and the number of its admirers has increased.

KODARUMANISHIKI (The Minor Dharma Brocade). *See Color Plate 7.* The plant named Kodarumanishiki was developed from Kodaruma, one of the taiwanchiku group, and it was registered in 1971. This is one of the newer varieties and is quite popular.

The leaf shape resembles its ancestor, Kodaruma, and thus it is small and drooping, with a slightly twisted curl. The leaf has beautiful small white stripes all over the surface. This pattern has a different sort of beauty and effect when compared with Zuishonishiki or Koganenishiki, which were also derived from Kodaruma. Kodarumanishiki has a high ornamental value.

The plant is very strong and easy to grow. There is very little irregularity in the stripe pattern. This variety has a high ability to multiply. For these reasons, Kodarumanishiki is expected to increase in favor with kansochiku enthusiasts.

KODARUMANOSHIMA (The Minor Dharma Stripes). This variety was derived from Kodaruma and was registered in 1975. It has clear, beautiful stripes, some broad and others narrow. Its small leaves are thick and drooping, and their twisting ends tend to split. The short, thick trunk gives the plant a dwarfed appearance.

Among kannonchiku, Kodaruma has the highest rate of multiplication, and Kodarumanoshima has inherited this characteristic. However, new shoots often do not retain the stripe pattern of the parent. As a result, plants with good stripes are not common.

KOGANENISHIKI (Gold Coin Brocade). Koganenishiki is a recent variety that developed from Kodaruma, a member of the taiwan-chiku group, and was registered in 1972. The small, thick leaves curl slightly and droop. The leafstalk is thick and short. This is a rather small, but beautiful, variety.

The stripe pattern develops as follows: when the leaf starts to come out, it has greenish-yellow stripes. Then the color of the stripes gradually changes into a beautiful gold. This variety has high ornamental value and is expected to become very popular in the future.

The plant is strong, much like Kodaruma, and easy to propagate because it has a strong multiplication capacity.

KOTOBUKI (Felicitations). *See Color Plate 17.* Kotobuki is a variety that appeared as a new shoot from Fukuju, which belongs to the native group. This variety was discovered during World War II, propagated for a few years, and registered in 1954. Since that time, this plant has gained great popularity as a rare variety. Today it is popular as one of the middle-grade varieties among the striped plants.

The stripes develop as follows: when the leaf starts to come out, the whole leaf shows a greenish color and the stripes are not evident. Later the stripes gradually appear and change from light green to clear yellowish-white. The plant's characteristic drooping leaf, the tip of which gently curls under, is unique.

The plant is very strong and easy to grow. However, although new shoots are produced readily, it is not common to find new ones having nice stripes. The plants that do have a good stripe pattern tend to be weak, so it is not easy to multiply them. The nicely patterned plants are in great demand because they are very rare.

MANGETSUNOSHIMA (Full Moon Stripes). This variety is a striped sport of the all-green Mangetsu. It was registered in 1974. The very small speckled stripes spread over the leaf surface seem like delicate white threads.

The big leaves are thick. The leaf surface is very smooth, with a beautiful luster. The plant is strong and easy to grow. However, a rather low percentage of its new shoots retain the desired pattern of variegation. As a result, Mangetsunoshima is scarce and highly sought after at present.

NANZANNISHIKI (Southern Moutain Brocade). *See Color Plate 15.* Nanzannishiki was discovered in Taiwan and then introduced into Japan. It is one of the newer varieties and was registered in 1970. Beautifully clear, yellow-white fine stripes appear all over the leaf on a deep green background. The leaf is large and thick, with a pleasing appearance.

The plant is quite strong and easy to propagate. There is little irregularity in the stripe pattern, and its ability to multiply is very high. The charm of this variety is enhanced by its aristocratic bearing.

NIKKODEN (Sun Ray Hall). *See Color Plate 23.* Nikkoden was developed from a kannonchiku plant belonging to the native group. When it was discovered that the cultivar Kinkoraku consisted of two different varieties, these were separated and designated as Ogonmaru and Nikkoden. Both were registered in 1966.

Clear yellow-white fine stripes appear on a deep green background. When the leaf first comes out, the stripe pattern is not very definite due to the greenish color of the whole leaf. Later the stripes become clear and yellow-white in color.

The plant is very strong and easy to cultivate. However, because the pattern tends to become rather irregular, nicely patterned plants are somewhat rare and much in demand.

OGONMARU (Gold Circle). Ogonmaru is a variety that developed from Kinkoraku, of the native group. Kinkoraku, a striped type of kannonchiku, has been in existence for a very long time. It was eventually found that among Kinkoraku there were two different types: one has light green stripes on a deep green leaf, together with clear deep yellow stripes; the other has clear whitish-yellow stripes and clear deep yellow stripes. These two varieties were distinguished in 1966. The former was designated as Ogonmaru, and the latter was called Nikkoden.

The stripe pattern is not clearly visible when the leaf starts to come out and is still a yellow-green color. However, the leaf gradually develops clear gold-colored stripes. The plant is very strong and easy to grow. However, it is difficult to find new shoots that have a nice stripe pattern, and as a result Ogonmaru is still a somewhat scarce variety.

Shihonoshima (Great Striped Treasure). Shihonoshima was derived from Shiho, which is one of the taiwanchiku group. This is a relatively new variety, having been registered in 1966.

The appearance of the leaf is pleasing. It is round, thick, and large, with an outstanding stripe pattern. Beautiful milk-white stripes appear all over the leaf. The leaf is very glossy and elegant, and therefore the plant has very high ornamental value.

Shihonoshima is expected to become a popular variety in the future, and proliferation of this variety is now in progress. However, the number of plants is still very small, and it is very rarely found in the average collection.

Shirotaenishiki (White Cloth Brocade). *See Color Plate 9.* Shirotaenishiki was derived from Hakkokinshi, which belongs to the taiwanchiku group, and it was registered in 1962.

The leaf is big and thick. The leafstalk is also thick. Extremely fine stripes as well as wide, clear stripes, appear all over the leaf. The stripe pattern is very beautiful and contributes to the high ornamental value of the plant. It is a rare but popular variety.

The plant is very strong and easy to grow, and it readily produces new plants. However, a nicely patterned plant is very unusual because the stripe pattern of this variety often becomes irregular. This challenge adds to the popularity of the plant.

Showanishiki (Showa Brocade). A number of valuable striped varieties have been developed from Tenzan, including Tenzanshiroshima, Tenzannoshima, and this plant, which was registered in 1974. However, Showanishiki has a distinctive type of variegation. As the new leaf opens, very clear snow-white stripes are seen. Gradually, after additional leaves grow, the stripes on the older leaves turn light green, beginning at the leaf tips. Finally, each entire leaf becomes green. The leaf is large, giving a massive, sturdy appearance to the plant. The contrast of the light stripes on newer leaves to the all-green older leaves is striking. To improve Showanishiki's white blush, use lower levels of light, temperature, and nitrogen in the fertilizer.

Showanishiki is an elegant plant that has rapidly become very popular. It is a strong grower, and few of the leaves have enough light area to cause any risk of damage from strong sunlight. This variety multiplies readily, and thus, although it is rather rare now, we can expect to see many of these plants in the future.

SHOZANNISHIKI (Shining Mountain Brocade). Registered in 1974, Shozannishiki was, like Darumanoshima, derived from the all-green variety Daruma. The two striped varieties are characterized by quite different development. When Darumanoshima first opens a new leaf, the stripe pattern is clearly visible. However, when Shozannishiki opens its new leaves, the stripe pattern is obscured and is greenish in color. Later the stripes become yellow and eventually turn a beautiful clear gold color.

The nicely shaped leaves have a slim width, since the frond readily splits into several leaflets. The leaf is thick and drooping, with a lustrous appearance. The trunk is short and thick, and the plant gives a strong but dwarfed impression. The stripes are wide, and care is needed to prevent damage from sunlight that is too intense.

TENMANISHIKI (Heavenly Brocade). *See Color Plate 10.* Tenmanishiki belongs to the taiwanchiku group. Produced from a variegated kannonchiku plant from Taiwan, it was registered in 1957.

This variety has beautiful clear yellow-white stripes that appear on a deep green background. The appearance of the leaf is attractive and very grand. The leaf is thick, and the leafstalk is thick and short. Tenmanishiki is highly ornamental and in great demand. Although the plant is strong and easily grown, it is very difficult to get a perfectly patterned new plant.

TENSHI (Gift from Heaven). Tenshi was derived from Tenzan, which is of Taiwanese origin. Registered in 1972, it is a large plant with drooping leaves that are very similar in their stripe pattern to Tenzanshiroshima. Tenshi's leaves are narrower and thinner, and the stripes are a clear yellow color. As new leaves emerge, they tend to split and spread like a person's hand. The contrast between the bright yellow stripes and the dark green is very beautiful. The attractive shape of the leaves greatly enhances the value of this variety.

Tenshi is a strong plant and easy to grow. However, care must be used to avoid too intense light. It is quite easy to burn the leaves of a plant with wide yellow stripes. Tenshi does not readily produce new shoots with a good stripe pattern.

TENZANNOSHIMA (Heavenly Mountain Stripes). *See Color Plate 2.* Tenzannoshima was derived from a popular all-green variety, Tenzan, which is one of the taiwanchiku-group plants. Tenzannoshima was registered in 1965 and is one of the highest grades among the popular varieties.

The stripe pattern consists of clear yellow stripes on a deep green background. The appearance of the leaf is attractive and gives a feeling of power and great size.

Tenzannoshima is strong and easy to grow, but the leaf pattern often becomes irregular, as can happen with many other striped kannonchiku plants. A rapid increase of this variety cannot be expected; however, since nicely patterned plants are very rare, the demand for Tenzannoshima is growing.

Many people still recall the early success of Tenzannoshima as soon as it was discovered in 1961, which resulted in a kannonchiku boom. From that time on, this plant has proliferated. However, it is still one of the rarest high-quality varieties of striped kannonchiku, and it is widely admired among kansochiku fans.

TENZANSHIROSHIMA (Heavenly Mountain White Stripes). *See Color Plate 1.* Tenzanshiroshima was derived from Tenzan, as was Tenzannoshima. Both varieties belong to the taiwanchiku group. Tenzanshiroshima was registered in 1967.

A special feature of Tenzanshiroshima is that it shows whitish-yellow stripes on the leaf. The stripe pattern is relatively clear when the leaf starts to come out. By comparison, the stripe pattern of Tenzannoshima is not clear when the leaf first opens, but later the stripes become light greenish and clear. The white stripe pattern of Tenzanshiroshima is bright and beautiful on the large-sized leaf. As a result, it has very high ornamental value. Today this variety is more popular than Tenzannoshima. Because the pattern readily becomes irregular, well-patterned plants are very rare and highly prized by kansochiku enthusiasts.

TOKAINISHIKI (Eastern Sea Brocade). *See Color Plate 14.* Tokainishiki is a typical popular variety of striped kannonchiku plant. It was discovered in the collection of a grower living in Aichi Prefecture who then began propagating it. This variety was registered in 1958. Although it is not clear to which group it belongs, judging from the appearance of the leaf, it is probably of taiwan-chiku origin.

The stripes are yellow-white, clear, and fine, appearing on a deep green background. The leaf is thick, the leafstalk is thick and short, and the trunk is thick. The vertical distance between leafstalks is short. This is a truly attractive variety with high ornamental value. At present, Tokainishiki is gaining popularity as one of the highest quality rare varieties, along with Tenzannoshima and Darumano-shima.

The plant is very strong and easy to grow. Irregularity in the pattern is relatively rare, and thus the chances of producing plants like the parent are good.

TOYONISHIKI (Oriental Brocade). *See Color Plate 11.* Toyonishiki is one of the newer varieties in the taiwanchiku group. Since it was discovered in the Mikawa district of Aichi Prefecture in 1962, it has been well propagated, and the plant was registered in 1970.

The appearance of the leaf resembles that of Zuikonishiki but is more regal. The leaf is thick, and the leafstalk is thick and short. The stripe pattern is clear, with pure white, extremely fine stripes all over the leaf. Additional characteristics include hairs on the base of the leaf and rough notches on the leaf's periphery.

The plant is strong and easy to grow. There is little irregularity in the stripe pattern, and the plant is known for its a good multi-plication rate.

UCHUDEN (Cosmos Hall). Uchuden was developed from one of the so-called native-group plants and was registered in 1949. It has the characteristic leaf shape and pattern of striped kannonchiku plants.

When the plant is young, the leaf of Uchuden has a broad shape, and it seldom splits. The tip of the leaf is very sharp, much like the tip of an Oriental writing brush. Every leaf has several yellow stripes in the middle portion of the leaf.

Uchuden has a distinctive leaf shape and pattern. It seldom shows any irregularity in its variegation, although the leaf patterns of most of the striped kannonchiku plants tend to be irregular.

Uchuden has a strong multiplication capacity, but its vigor is a little lower than average. Therefore, some people feel that the cultivation of this plant is not easy. During the summertime, care must be taken to avoid exposing the plant to strong sunlight; it should be kept in a cool and well-ventilated place. In the wintertime, be sure to keep the plant warm and avoid giving it too much fertilizer.

ZUIKONISHIKI (Auspicious Light Brocade). *See Color Plate 20.* Zuikonishiki was derived from a native-group plant, Kinshi, and maintains the top position as a popular representative variety of variegated kannonchiku plants.

Pure white, fine stripes appear all over the leaf. The contrast between white and green is exquisite, and this variety has very high ornamental value.

The plant is very strong and easy to grow and also readily forms new shoots. Since there is very little irregularity in the stripe pattern, this plant has a good multiplication rate.

In the striped category of kannonchiku plants, this variety has been loved throughout many decades by all kinds of growers of kansochiku plants, from beginners to veterans.

ZUISHONISHIKI (Good Omen Brocade). *See Color Plate 6.* Zuishonishiki was derived from a popular variety, Kodaruma, and was registered in 1959.

The size of the leaf is small but pleasing in appearance. The leafstalk is short and gives a dwarflike appearance to the plant. Very fine, pure white stripes appear over most of the leaf surface, giving the plant an interesting leaf pattern. The leaves have very little luster.

The plant is rather weak and not so easy for beginners to grow, but it has a high ornamental value.

IRREGULARLY SPOTTED KANNONCHIKU

CHOYO (Trillion Suns). *See Color Plate 27.* Choyo belongs to the taiwanchiku group and was registered in 1949 during one of the revival periods of kansochiku plants after World War II. It was a popular variety in those days.

The leaf is big and thick. Beautiful softly outlined spots, which are at first white and then become yellowish, appear all over the leaf.

Choyo is robust and grows very fast. It has a high capacity for multiplying. The plant can be grown even by a beginner and is therefore very popular.

DARUMANOZU (Dharma's Picture). This variety was developed from Daruma, which belongs to the taiwanchiku group, and was registered in 1963. There are clear white spots all over the leaf.

The plant has glossy, thick, drooping leaves, many of which split at the ends. This is the most beautiful and popular variety among the spotted kannonchiku plants.

Darumanozu is very strong. However, it is very sensitive to intense light, and like other spotted kannonchiku the leaf easily gets sunburned. It has a good capacity for multiplying and makes many new shoots. Moreover, there is little irregularity in the pattern on the leaf.

HAGOROMONOZU (Feathered Cape Picture). Hagoromonozu was developed from Hagoromo, which belongs to the taiwanchiku group. Clear white spots appear on the leaf. The plant was registered in 1935.

The appearance of the leaf resembles that of Fukuju. The leaf is narrow and drooping. The leafstalk is short, and the leaf splits easily.

Hagoromonozu is vigorous and grows very rapidly. It has a high multiplication rate and produces many new shoots. This is a suitable variety for beginners.

KINSEIKO (Starlight Brocade). Kinseiko was introduced to Japan from Taiwan and now belongs among the popular varieties. The leaves are big and thick, and the leafstalk is thick and short, making Kinseiko an attractively compact plant.

Blurred, snakeskin-like spots spread diffusely all over the leaf. However, this variegation is not observed in all plants of this variety; some of them exhibit no spots and have entirely green leaves.

The plant is very strong and easy to grow. It grows very fast and has a high capacity to multiply.

MANGETSUNOZU (Full Moon Picture). Mangetsunozu developed when clear, beautiful spots appeared on the leaves of a specimen of Mangetsu (a popular variety of the taiwanchiku group) and remained stable. This new variety was registered in 1970.

The attractive leaf is large and glossy, with a smooth surface. Mangetsunozu is very strong and easy to grow and has a good capacity to multiply.

MEISEI (Fame). Meisei was derived from a variety that was introduced from Taiwan. It was registered in 1957.

Meisei has beautiful spots all over the leaf. The spots are white when the leaves first open, and they then gradually develop a yellow-white color. Sometimes long and thin marks, which look like vertical stripes, delicately appear on the leaf.

The plant is very strong and easy to propagate. It has a strong ability to produce new shoots.

SHORYU (Ascending Dragon). Shoryu was introduced to Japan from abroad and registered in 1953. It belongs to the imported group.

The leaf is narrow in shape and splits easily. Clear yellow-white spots that have blurred outlines appear on a deep green background all over the leaf.

The plant is not very vigorous, and in fact it is a rather weak grower. Shoryu should not be overfertilized or exposed to strong sunlight. However, if the light intensity is too low, the spots become faint or ambiguous, and the ornamental value of the plant declines. Proper lighting, although difficult to achieve, is very important for this delicate plant. Growers thus consider Shoryu a worthy challenge to their expertise.

TORYUMON (Gateway to Success). Toryumon belongs to the rakanchiku group of plants. It was very popular during the period of increasing interest in kansochiku plants after World War II. Greenish-white spots appear on a deep green background all over the leaf. These spots are round, and inside them appear smaller green dots, which growers say resemble a dragon's eye.

The plant is very strong and is easy to grow. It has a high capacity for multiplying and produces many new shoots.

AIKOKUDEN (Hall of Patriotism). Aikokuden belongs to the taiwanchiku group and was registered in 1957. Its large, wide leaves are thick and drooping. The leaf has a tendency to bend gradually from the middle to the tip.

This variety is characterized by a deep green color and a lusterless appearance of the leaves. The plant is graceful and solid and highly ornamental.

The shape of the leaf of Aikokuden is very similar to that of Keigetsu, and many people confuse the two varieties. However, compared with Keigetsu, Aikokuden has a deeper green and lusterless woolly texture to the leaf, and the leaf is thicker and hangs downward more.

The plant is healthy and easy to grow. It has a strong ability to produce new shoots.

DAIFUKUDEN (Great Fortune Hall). The leaves of Daifukuden are very big, wide, and thick, in keeping with its Taiwanese origin. Their appearance reminds some people of the bottom of a ship because the leaves are long and heavily ribbed. The plant grows rapidly, produces many new shoots, and is a fine choice for beginners.

DAIKOKUTEN (Fortune). Of Taiwanese origin, this plant is almost as popular as Tenzan and Koban. The large, rounded leaves are very wide and give the plant an appearance of size and strength that is quite attractive. Daikokuten is very prolific, easy to grow, and well suited for beginning growers of kannonchiku. A variegated form of the plant, Daikokutennoshima, has brilliant yellow stripes on its leaves.

DAIMYO (Lord). Daimyo resembles a larger version of Kodaruma. The leaf surfaces have a smooth, very glossy appearance, which makes the plant very ornamental. The plant is prolific and quite easy to grow.

DARUMA (Dharma). *See Color Plate 28*. Daruma is another plant in the taiwanchiku group and, like Tenzan and Koban, is very popular. The leaves are of high quality, being narrow but thick. The smooth leaves have a high gloss. The distance between nodes on the trunk, where the leafstalks are attached, is quite short. A prominent characteristic of Daruma is the splitting of each frond into many narrow leaflets like those of shurochiku. Daruma has an elegant appearance, giving the plant great ornamental and commercial value.

Its fast rate of growth and its ability to produce many new shoots make Daruma a good selection for a beginner. The variegated forms of this plant are named Darumanoshima and Darumanozu. Both of these are also very popular.

FUKIDEN (Rich Noble Hall). Of Taiwanese ancestry, Fukiden was registered in 1963. The attractive leaves are very thick, and their shape is short and wide. The leafstalks are thick, and their vertical spacing on the trunk is short. This beautiful plant is very popular for its ornamental value. Fukiden is comparatively slow growing, but produces a good number of new plants. It is a good choice for beginners.

FUKUJU (Lucky Felicitations). This very popular plant has a relatively long history, having been discovered in the 1930s. It is probably one of the native-group plants. The leaves are medium-sized, thin, and drooping. The leaf tips curve gradually toward the center of the plant.

Fukuju is easy to care for, grows very rapidly, and readily produces many new shoots. Beginners do well with this plant. Variegated cultivars derived from Fukuju include Kotobuki, Hakuju, and Choju, all of which are very popular.

GYOKUHO (Precious Treasure). *See Color Plate 33.* Gyokuho belongs to the taiwanchiku group and was introduced from Taiwan. Whereas most taiwanchiku-group varieties are big, Gyokuho is exceptional for its small size.

The shape of the leaf is rounded and small, and the leafstalk is thick and short. The leaf is resistant to splitting. This is a pretty and popular variety.

The plant is a good grower and easy to propagate. It has a strong capacity for producing new shoots.

17. Kotobuki

18. Kannonchikushima

19. Hakuhonishiki

20. Zuikonishiki

21. Chiyodazuru

22. Akatsuki

23. Nikkoden

24. Hakutsurunishiki   25. Ayanishiki

26. Hakuju

27. Choyo

28. Daruma

29. Kodaruma

30. Himedaruma

31. Gyokuryu

32. Shiho

33. Gyokuho

34. Koban

35. Towaden

36. Mangetsu

37. Keigetsu

SHUROCHIKU

38. Shurochikushima

39. Kinsho

40. Hakuseiden

41. *Nishiki*-style pots

GYOKURYU (Precious Dragon). *See Color Plate 31.* Gyokuryu belongs to the taiwanchiku group. The leaf is thick and narrow, and it splits easily. There are vertical lines or folds, which resemble waves, all over the leaf. The leaf does not droop but remains in an upward direction, giving a sturdy image to the plant.

The plant is vigorous and easy to grow. It readily produces new shoots.

HEIWADEN (Peace Hall). Heiwaden belongs to the taiwanchiku group of plants. If Taiheiden bears the title of king of the all-green kannonchiku, then Heiwaden is surely the queen. The beautiful leaves are very big, wide, and round in shape. The leaf is very thin, with a smooth, shiny appearance. The shape of the leaves accounts for Heiwaden's great popularity and ornamental value. The plants grow rapidly and multiply quickly.

HIMEDARUMA (Princess Dharma). *See Color Plate 30.* This cultivar was discovered before World War II, so it is relatively old. The thin, high-quality leaves hang downward, and the tips are curved toward the trunk a little, giving a beautiful overall appearance. Another plant, Otohime, is often confused with Himedaruma. The difference is that the leaf tips of Otohime do not curl inward, but are relatively straight. Himedaruma is a fast grower, reproduces readily, and is well suited for beginners.

Ho-o (Phoenix). This variety belongs to the imported group. The leaves of Ho-o are split finely into narrow segments. Their downward orientation reminds people of the feathers of the mythical phoenix. This elegant plant grows quite rapidly, multiplies readily, and is easy for beginners. However, Ho-o has recently become hard to find.

KEIGETSU (Benevolent Moon). *See Color Plate 37.* Keigetsu belongs to the taiwanchiku group and was originally known as Aikokuden. Eventually a difference was found among the Aikokuden plants. The new type of plant was separated from Aikokuden, designated as Keigetsu, and registered in 1965. It has a very short history since its discovery as a new variety, but it is now widely distributed and very popular.

The leaf is large and drooping, and its shape resembles that of Aikokuden. However, Keigetsu has a thinner leaf and a smoother and more lustrous leaf surface.

The plant is robust and easy to propagate. It has a strong tendency to multiply, and it readily makes new shoots.

KOBAN (Gold Coin). *See Color Plate 34.* Koban is one of the taiwanchiku-group plants. Along with Tenzan and Daruma, Koban is one of the most popular all-green kannonchiku cultivars. The shape of the leaf is very pleasing, and its rounded appearance suggests the reason for the plant's name. The leaves have little tendency to split, and their shape is short, wide, and drooping. The distance between leafstalks on the trunk is very short, giving the plant an attractive shape. Koban is widely used as an ornamental plant. It is very prolific and easy to grow, making it a fine choice for beginners. A variegated sport, Kobannishiki, is also very popular.

KODARUMA (Minor Dharma). *See Color Plate 29.* Kodaruma belongs to the taiwanchiku group. The thick leaf is small, drooping, and slightly twisted. The leafstalk is thick and short.

The plant is sturdy and easy to propagate. It easily produces new shoots, more so than any other kannonchiku plants. Kodaruma does not develop any abnormal elongation of the trunk, and thus the distance between joints is short. As a result, it is easy for beginners to cultivate this plant without any deterioration of its attractive shape.

From this variety, Koganenishiki, Kodarumanishiki, and Zuishonishiki have been developed.

MANGETSU (Full Moon). *See Color Plate 36.* Another plant of Taiwanese extraction, Mangetsu is very popular, along with Heiwaden and Taiheiden. The quality of the large, shiny leaves is good. The leaves are thick, with smooth surfaces. Round and beautiful, the leaves remind the viewer of *mangetsu,* the full moon. This very ornamental plant is easy to grow and quite prolific.

NAMIKANNONCHIKU (All-green Kannonchiku). This is a very old type. Having appeared in Japan during the Edo period (1603–

1868), it is considered the native-group ancestor of a number of kannonchiku cultivars. The leaf is rather thin, and it tends to split readily into narrow segments. Namikannonchiku grows rapidly, produces many new shoots, and is quite suitable for beginners to propagate.

OTOHIME (Younger Princess). Otohime was derived from the imported group. It has one of the smallest leaves among kannonchiku varieties, and the leaf is characterized by a small, narrow, and pointed tip. The leaf is thick.

The shape of the leaf strongly resembles that of Himedaruma, which belongs to the same category of kannonchiku plants, so people often confuse the two varieties. However, unlike Himedaruma, Otohime is characterized by leaf tips that curl inward.

The plant is strong and easy to cultivate. It has a strong multiplication capacity. If properly grown, Otohime has a unique, highly ornamental appearance. This is a suitable variety for the beginner.

SHIHO (Treasures). *See Color Plate 32.* Shiho is in the taiwanchiku group, and its rounded leaves are of high quality. The shape of the large leaves is short and wide, and they are very shiny in appearance. The drooping contour of the leaves gives this beautiful plant great ornamental value. Recently a variegated form of this plant has been found and is called Shihonoshima.

SHIPPODEN (Seven Treasure Hall). Also of Taiwanese origin, Shippoden was registered in 1963, so it is among the newer kannonchiku varieties. The quality of the leaf shape is very good: large-sized and with a drooping appearance. The juvenile leaves that first form have very little tendency to split. Its wide leaves make this a very ornamental plant. The plant is easy to grow, readily produces new shoots, and is a good choice for beginners.

TAIHEIDEN (Peace Hall). Taiheiden is perhaps the most popular of the all-green plants. Imported from Taipei before World War II and registered in 1949, it is characterized as the "king of kannonchiku." It was discovered as a sport among other taiwanchiku-group plants. The quality of the leaf is very good, being large, wide, and thick. The leaves are relatively short, and the leafstalks are very thick. This noble plant is very ornamental, but compared to other cultivars it grows rather slowly. However, it is easy to grow and produces many new shoots.

TENZAN (Heavenly Mountain). This variety is of Taiwanese origin and, together with Koban and Daruma, enjoys great popularity. The name Tenzan came from a Japanese naval jet plane that was used in World War II. The high-quality leaves have a tendency to droop, and they are very wide and large, with little splitting.

Tenzan is popular for its ornamental value. It grows fast, readily produces many new plants, and is a good choice for beginners. Variegated forms are Tenzannoshima and Tenzanshiroshima. Both are of the finest quality and very much in demand.

TOWADEN (Oriental Hall). *See Color Plate 35.* Towaden is in the taiwanchiku group, derived from the very popular cultivar Heiwaden. A recent introduction, Towaden was registered in 1971. The leaves are extremely large and wide, and they slope gracefully downward. An outstanding feature of the leaf is that it has very little tendency to split. Its beauty places the plant among the highest ranks of all-green cultivars. It grows very fast, produces many new shoots, and is easy to grow.

SHUROCHIKU

HAKUMEIJO (Bright White Castle). Derived from the all-green Shurochikuao, Hakumeijo is a plant with an unusual "splash" pattern on its leaves. This rare plant is hard to find offered for sale. The frond is finely divided into many narrow leaflets, which hang down gracefully. The plant grows rapidly, but like Kimboshi it is easily sunburned by too intense light.

HAKUSEIDEN (Green and White Hall). *See Color Plate 40.* This is another of the variegated sports which appeared from the all-green Shurochikuao. It was registered in 1955 and rapidly achieved the highest rank because of its beauty and rarity. The shape of the leaflets is very narrow, and the finely split frond slopes downward very gracefully. On most leaflets there are bright white stripes, and the contrast between these and the beautiful green makes this elegant plant much desired by all who see it. Hakuseiden grows very fast and easily develops new shoots. But if the plant has a considerable amount of white on its leaves, care must be taken to avoid too much light, or the leaves are likely to burn.

KIMBOSHI (Gold Star). This is a variegated plant that appeared as a mutation of the all-green Shurochikuao. It has small round yellowish-white dots on the leaves. When they first emerge, the leaves are mostly white, but as they mature green color gradually develops. This cultivar is rare and seldom seen. The plant is very easy to propagate, for it grows quickly. Because of the light-colored spots, the leaves are easily sunburned, so the plant should not be exposed to intense light.

KINSHO (Pine Brocade). *See Color Plate 39.* Kinsho is a variegated sport or mutation of the all-green Shurochikuao. It was registered in 1940. The orientation of the leaves is interesting because of the upright stance given to the plant. All of the leaves have very fine white stripes on every part of their surfaces. Many people admire and appreciate the special ornamental qualities of Kinsho, so it still retains its popularity. It is rather weak growing and is thus hard for beginners to handle correctly. The plant should be kept in a relatively cool, well-ventilated place in summer. In winter, the plant needs a warm spot. It must not be overfertilized.

SHUROCHIKUAO (Green-leaf Shurochiku). This variety is also called Namishurochiku, and it has long been a popular plant in Japan. The beautiful leaves hang downward, giving the plant an elegant, attractive appearance. Shurochikuao is very adaptable to cold weather. It grows rapidly and easily produces new shoots. Compared to kannonchiku, Shurochikuao is not as prolific in its production of new shoots. It is used not only as a potted plant, but also as a garden specimen planted in the ground.

SHUROCHIKUSHIMA (Shurochiku Stripes). *See Color Plate 38.* Shurochikushima is a variegated plant derived by a mutation from the all-green Shurochikuao. It has beautiful white-to-yellow stripes on nearly all of the leaves. When the leaves first emerge, they are light green, with just a hint of yellow stripes. Later, the stripes are more obvious, but lighter in color. The quality of the leaves is very high, with rather pale green leaflets of an elegant drooping shape. The many narrow leaflets spread out like a fan. The plant grows very fast and multiplies readily, although not as much as kannon-chiku. This variety surely deserves its great popularity.

5

Selecting Kansochiku

The first thing to have in mind is one's purposes in raising these palms. Some people grow kansochiku because they admire the plants and appreciate their decorative value. Others propagate them professionally, and still others do it as a business on the side to supplement their incomes.

This book introduces eighty of the approximately one hundred named varieties of kansochiku. Most kansochiku, as has been said before, are very sturdy, easy-to-raise plants. Prices range from about $10 to $2,000, and thus many of the plants can be bought at reasonable cost. Most are relatively inexpensive, but because of the wide price range, beginners often have a hard time knowing which plants to try first.

WHAT TO LOOK FOR

An expensive kansochiku plant is impractical for beginners. If something should go wrong with a valuable plant, the loss can be heavy. The expensive ones are also more difficult to care for, and a beginner who starts with an expensive plant runs a higher risk of failure.

Beginners should choose one of the less expensive varieties with solid green leaves. In addition to being cheaper, such plants are easier to raise, and they have a higher reproduction rate than the variegated types. In this way, a beginner can learn daily care, fertilizing, and watering methods. Having become familiar with cultivation techniques, then the novice may try acquiring more expensive plants.

Variegated kansochiku plants may have stripes that will change as the plants grow. Sometimes when a plant is young it is considered perfect, which means that the alternating white and green stripes are distinct and of equal size. Often, however, as the plant grows the new leaves will change, and the stripes may become less defined or may merge together. It is also important to realize that the young shoots of a parent plant do not necessarily turn out looking the same as the original.

Examples of variegated plants in the medium price range are: Zuikonishiki, Kotobuki, Kinsho, Hinodenishiki, Shurochikushima, Kannonchikushima, and Chiyodazuru. Some of the most expensive plants are Eizannishiki, Nanzannishiki, Hakuseiden, Darumanoshima, Tenzanshiroshima, Tokainishiki, and Daikokutennoshima.

How to Obtain Kansochiku

Kansochiku plants are widely available in Japan through nurseries, specialized dealers, department stores, and amateur exchange clubs, so residents of Japan can easily acquire kansochiku. Readers in Japan wishing any further information may contact the Kansokai (Japan Kansochiku Association) at 74–2 Shironishi, Soraku, Kizucho, Soraku-gun, Kyoto-fu 612–02, Japan.

Readers outside Japan may obtain information concerning kansochiku availability by writing the co-author, J. Leland Hollenberg, at his mail-order nursery: Unilab Products, P.O. Box 84, Redlands, California 92373. Joining the Palm Society, P.O. Box 368, Lawrence, Kansas 66044, will provide further introductions to people with extra plants or other sources.

When purchasing through mail order, buyers cannot choose the plants they want, and it is up to the dealer which plant to send. Of course it is to no advantage to the dealer to sell someone a poor plant because of the effect this would have on his reputation. However, when buying a variegated kansochiku through the mail, it is unusual to get exactly the plant desired. When it is to be mailed, unless it is a valuable kind, the plant will probably be pulled out of the pot and the roots wrapped with moist sphagnum moss for ship-

Young shoots often vary in stripe pattern.

A short plant with wide leaves is the best choice.

ment. This is quite satisfactory for orders during favorable weather, when risk of freezing is minimal. Valuable plants are usually shipped in the pot.

The best way to use mail order is first to buy an all-green kansochiku to acquire experience growing this type of plant. Then when advancing to better striped varieties, it is advisable to visit the dealer directly. If a visit is not possible, at least be sure to check the grade of the plant being purchased. Typical grades are "average," "better," and "choice."

CHOOSING A GOOD PLANT

It is not easy for beginners to make good selections among plants. Generally, traders or nurseries deal with plants of various ages. Some are small shoots that have just been separated from the parent plant, and others are larger shoots that already have their own tiny new shoots emerging. There are also more mature plants that are firmly rooted and have well-developed new shoots.

THE BEST PLANTS FOR BEGINNERS Beginners would do better to avoid buying young shoots that are not yet well established. Best would be shoots that have been removed from the parent plant long enough to recover from the shock of the separation and transplanting. These grow vigorously, and they are easy to raise.

More mature plants are another possibility. However, they can be expensive, and they will produce new shoots, which may need to be separated soon. Separation of the young shoots is not easy for beginners, and it is helpful to have some experienced person demonstrate the technique the first time.

KANSOCHIKU FOR DECORATIVE PURPOSES Be sure not to buy very young shoots if the intention is purely decorative. Other than that, there are no particular restrictions. Tall plants or those with many young shoots in a pot look best in large rooms. Small and single-stem plants are suitable for table decoration or placement near a window.

JUDGING PLANT QUALITY It is very hard to determine the quality of a plant just by looking at it. With some experience, judgement

Avoid leaves burned by too much sunshine.

can sometimes be made based on the color and appearance of the leaves. However, this is difficult for most people. The easiest way is of course to ask the dealer, but there is in fact one simple indication of the quality of the plant that even beginners can use. If the roots are protruding from the bottom hole of the pot, the plant is likely to be a vigorously growing specimen that has recovered from the damage of the separation process. The roots can reveal both the condition and the age of the plant. (See pages 52, 67, and 70.)

HINTS FOR SELECTION

1. Choose a plant whose leaves are shiny and healthy looking. The luster of the leaves indicates the health condition of the plant, just as the skin reflects the condition of the human body. Healthy plants have lustrous leaves. If the leaves are extremely dark green, the plant has been raised in a shady location and may not be healthy. A plant that has been raised in bright sunshine will have a slight yellowish cast to its green leaves. Avoid buying a plant that has leaves burned by too much sunshine.

Examine for insect damage.

2. Select a plant with new leaves. A healthy plant has many new leaves coming out, like a Japanese fan. However, there are some plants with new leaves that seem to have stopped growing. This condition is caused by cold weather during winter, or it may indicate that these plants have not received good care. Be careful not to purchase such plants.

3. Choose a short plant with many short and wide leaves and a thick stem at the base. Such a plant will produce many new healthy shoots.

4. Avoid buying a plant that has damaged leaves. Kansochiku are very strong plants, and it is unusual for them to be injured by insects. But if they are raised in a greenhouse, infection may spread from other plants.

Scale insects and the brown spot fungus are the most common diseases (see pages 101–4). Unfortunately, even if the plants are sprayed when such problems are noticed, the scars on the leaves will remain.

Avoid buying plants with a burned appearance at the tips of the leaves. This problem usually indicates something wrong with the roots.

5. Select plants with roots that are dense and well grown. With the pot in one hand, hold the base of the trunk with the other hand. Now shake the trunk gently. If the trunk and roots feel unsteady, the plant is unhealthy.

Also look at the drainage hole of the pot. Healthy plants have long roots coming out of the hole, and the roots are white. Browned roots are an indication of a bad plant. The color of the tips of the leaves also shows the condition of the roots. If the tips are brown, the roots will be unhealthy.

The above five points should be kept in mind when picking solid green plants. The two points that follow will help in selecting variegated kansochiku.

6. Carefully study the stripe pattern on variegated plants. Avoid choosing those that have too great a striped or light-colored area on the leaves. The leaves of such plants burn too easily. Also, their new shoots tend to be very similar to the parent or will sometimes have all-white or light yellow leaves.

On the other hand, those that have almost no stripes on the leaves are inferior. Although this kind tends to be strong and healthy,

Test the plant with both hands for a steady trunk and a thickly packed root ball.

Long white roots extending from the drain hole are one indication of a healthy plant.

Too-white leaves are susceptible to burning.

nicely striped leaves will not necessarily appear on the new shoots. Solid green leaves may develop instead.

Plants having half white or yellow leaves with the other half solid green are considered less valuable. The same is true of those that have mostly striped leaves on one side of the plant and mainly solid leaves on the other. Plants with these defects tend to produce new shoots with irregularly striped leaves. It is possible for such inferior plants to produce beautiful new shoots, but this is rare. On the other hand, since such plants are less expensive but still grow readily, they can be good for beginners.

7. When buying variegated plants, try to choose the best and most expensive kinds. Generally, the stripe design tends to change as the plants grow. For example, the quantity of stripes tends to increase or decrease, a good stripe pattern becoming less attractive or vice versa. The better the quality of the plant, the less its stripe pattern is likely to change. Therefore, more expensive plants will always be a better investment in the long run, particularly since they are just as easy to take care of as the less attractively striped ones.

Sogara: every leaf has stripes.

Katagara: only a part of the plant has striped leaves.

Hangara: half of the leaves have stripes and half do not.

Hadegara: too many stripes make the leaf look white; the light part is greater than the green part.

Jimigara: stripes on the leaves can hardly be seen.

Genpeigara: half of a leaf is white and the other half is green.

Hakemejima: stripes that appear to be drawn by a brush; very thin stripes evenly stretching to the end of the leaf.

The best striped varieties have *sogara* and *hakemejima*.

Hangara.

Hadegara.

Jimigara.

Genpeigara.

Hakemejima.

6

Pots and Potting

SOIL

Plants usually carry on respiration not only with their leaves but also with their roots. Therefore, the soil should enhance the roots' ability to breathe. Any kind of soil is satisfactory, provided it allows water to drain easily, permits good aeration, retains enough moisture, and has a pH near six. Particularly because kansochiku are raised in partial shade or indoors, the most important requirements are good drainage and adequate soil ventilation. Meeting these conditions allows the roots to grow actively, avoids too vigorous plant growth, and gives the leaves an attractive appearance. Among commercial soils, the loose, coarse mix intended for African violets is most suitable. A bark mixture, moreover, requires less-frequent watering.

RIVER SAND   To satisfy the above conditions, people commonly use the coarse sand and gravel from a riverbed. Some people use pumice stones or packaged sands. When gathering sand from a river, be careful to adhere to the following:

1. Collect sand from the upper stream. It is better to use sand with angular grains rather than rounded ones, because the former retains more water and allows more air to move through the sand. Therefore, the sand from upstream, which has not lost its sharp angles by tumbling, is better than sand from the lower stream.

2. Use clean sand. Sand that has been used before to grow other plants is not suitable for use in growing kansochiku, because

Convenient commercial soils.

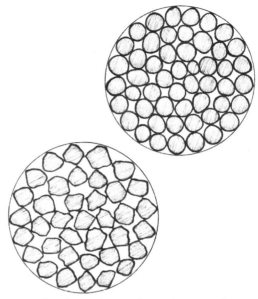

Angular grains are better than smooth for water and air circulation.

Collect river sand from the upper stream.

Sift sand into three sizes.

it often contains too much fertilizer or harmful microorganisms. These could affect the roots, and the plant may get infected.

It is best to use new sand from a river. However, if old sand is the only thing available, rinse and clean it thoroughly.

3. Remove the smallest fragments before use. Sift the sand with a fine strainer (with a mesh of about 1.5 millimeters) to remove the finest pieces. Then sift the remaining sand with a 3- to 4-millimeter strainer and again with a 5- to 6-millimeter strainer. These can be made by covering frames with 1/16–, 1/8–, and 1/4–inch mesh hardware cloth. The sand will thus be divided into three grades, with grains the size of beans, small peas, and rice, respectively.

Although the small fragments can be completely removed for kannonchiku, retain some of these fragments for shurochiku.

USING SPHAGNUM MOSS Even when good river sand is used for potting, the roots of a kansochiku plant may still become too dry occasionally. To prevent excessive drying, place some wet, coarse sphagnum moss on top of the sand. Sphagnum moss also helps keep the sand in place when the plant is watered.

SOIL NUTRIENTS Even when a kansochiku plant is grown perfectly, its green leaves can sometimes fade and turn yellow. This phenomenon is caused by a lack of certain minor chemical elements in the soil. Nitrogen, phosphorus, and potassium (N, P, and K) are well known to be essential major nutrients for the growth of plants. However, the minor elements including calcium, magnesium, iron, sulfur, and manganese are also necessary in lesser amounts. River sand usually has enough of these minor nutrients, so there is no need to provide additional amounts. When the same soil is used for years, when old sand is reused for planting new shoots, or when the pot is too small for the size of the plant, some of the essential elements may be lacking.

There are several solutions to this problem. The yellowing may be alleviated by adding some fertilizer to the soil, but it is preferable to replant in new soil as soon as possible. The regular use of a fertilizer that provides all of the minor chemical elements, as well as nitrogen, phosphorus, and potassium, helps prevent the soil from becoming depleted and thus keeps the leaves from fading.

Buy or make strainers of appropriate sizes.

Sand the size of rice, peas, and beans.

Prepare moss for a covering.

The most important requirement for a kansochiku pot is that water should drain well and that the pot should retain some moisture and allow air to enter freely. Many kinds of pots are sold at stores, in various colors, shapes, and sizes. The kansochiku pot does not need to be of a special type as long as it allows the plant to grow sufficiently. Some growers in Japan have attempted to adapt regular pots by drilling additional holes in the sides for better aeration, but this tends to dry out the roots too much.

In the United States, where Japanese kansochiku pots are still hard to find, plastic pots are used almost exclusively. Provided several additional drain holes are drilled in the bottom, plastic pots can be a very satisfactory alternative.

If the plants are not being grown for commercial purposes but for personal enjoyment, the shape and decoration of the pot are also important elements to consider. An unglazed pot, for example, can be both inexpensive and good for the plant, but its plainness causes the plant to lose some of its ornamental value. The elegance of the plant and the appearance of an inexpensive pot tend to conflict. Remember that the pot needs to suit both the growth and the beauty of the plant.

SPECIAL KANSOCHIKU POTS For these purposes, the special kansochiku pot is the best choice. Developed as a result of many years of effort and experience, it has proven to be suitable for growing kannonchiku and shurochiku plants as close to perfection as possible. (See Color Plate 41.)

Generally, there are two pot types. The *katayaki* pot is the less expensive, being machine made in large quantities. Practical and popular, this pot provides good ventilation and drainage. The hand-molded *rakuyaki* pot, on the other hand, requires much skill and time in the making and is much more expensive. Thin and fragile, its porous nature provides excellent aeration and drainage. Superior plant growth can also be expected from *rakuyaki* pots, the thin walls of which are better than *katayaki* at transmitting room heat to the soil.

Usually kansochiku pots are glazed and entirely black in color. This not only makes the plant look more attractive, but since the

Several pot sizes and shapes are suitable.

Katayaki *pot.*

Nishiki-*style pot.*

black color tends to absorb the heat from the sun, it also keeps the inside warm and is good for the growth of the roots, particularly in winter.

Pots decorated with beautiful designs or pictures, in contrast to those that are entirely black, are called *nishiki*-style pots. These elaborate pots can be divided into three categories. Those known simply as *nishiki* pots are typically decorated with pictures of dragons, lions, or flowers. These are the most expensive and are used to hold the most highly prized plants. Second most valuable are *naminishiki* pots, which have waves and birds drawn near the bottom. The most simple type is the *fuchikin* pot, the rim or legs of which are gold colored.

Although beautiful, *nishiki*-style pots are very expensive, and beginners would be well advised to wait awhile before purchasing them. *Nishiki* pots should contain plants worthy of their beauty.

Kansochiku pots are made deeper than ordinary pots. This prevents the roots from growing sideways and permits them to grow downward. In addition, there is a large hole at the bottom of the pot, and there are legs underneath. These features let the water drain better and make the pot more graceful. To keep the potting medium in place, the drain hole is covered with a special piece of ceramic called a *sana,* the most common of which is molded into a cupped shape and pierced with seven rather large holes.

POT SIZES   Pots suitable for kansochiku range in size from 9 to 24 centimeters (3.5–10 inches) in diameter across the rim. Small pots are better for the growth of the plants because the soil dries out faster. Small pots are also more attractive with miniature plants.

Beginners tend to use big pots in an attempt to grow more roots or to prevent rapid drying. This is a mistake. Small pots allow the roots to dry faster and let the air permeate the soil more quickly. As a result, plants in small pots grow more vigorously and have stronger roots.

Plants raised in big pots, on the other hand, do not need to develop strong roots to absorb water because of the greater amount of moisture in the soil. Even if some roots are produced, they will tend to rot because their respiration systems can be disturbed by too much water in the pot.

Usually a pot about 12 centimeters (5 inches) in diameter will

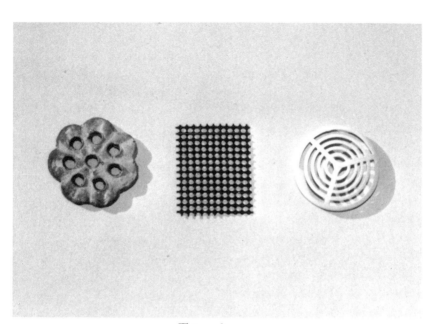

Types of sana.

A large hole for good drainage.

Choose a smaller, well-fitting pot suited to the size of the root ball.

be suitable for a new shoot that has just been separated from its parent plant. Large plants and those that have two or three new shoots may be all right in pots with a diameter of 15 to 18 centimeters (6–7 inches). If faced with a choice, always choose a somewhat smaller pot for the size of the plant rather than a larger one.

Because there are no special kansochiku pots bigger than 30 centimeters (12 inches), it will be necessary to use an ordinary large and deep plant pot when the palm is allowed to grow to full size for a room decoration. In this case, too, be careful to adhere to the preceding requirements regarding size, shape, color, and quality of the pot.

7

Propagation

Although it is very difficult to grow kansochiku from seeds and impossible from cuttings of the stem or leaf, separating the new shoots from the parent is an easy and suitable means of increasing the number of plants. A kansochiku plant, if it is well cared for, will usually have one to three new shoots each year coming out near its base. There are rarely many new shoots at one time, but a typical plant will produce a few of them regularly. Because the new shoots appear naturally from the original plant, it is not very difficult to propagate kansochiku.

WHEN TO SEPARATE

From May to June and from the middle of September to the beginning of October are the best seasons for separation of the new kansochiku shoots. In Japan, the rainy period that occurs in May and June makes this an ideal season, since both the temperature and humidity are high, providing good conditions for plant growth. At such times, the plants can recover quickly from the damage to the roots caused by the separation process. Furthermore, the roots will have time to develop sufficiently before summer, when the plants normally do most of their growing.

Even when the separation is done by experts, the roots are usually damaged to some extent. In particular, the tender ends of the roots are easily injured.

65

AVOID EXTREME TEMPERATURES Although kansochiku plants originated in a subtropical zone, they are relatively tolerant to cold. On the other hand, cold weather is not good for these plants. The temperature should be at least 10° C (50° F) in order to grow kansochiku. When the temperature drops below 10° C, the plants will not grow at their normal rate, and when it goes below 5° C (40° F), the plants stop growing altogether.

If the plants are separated under poor cultural conditions, they become weak rather quickly. Once the plants are weakened or damaged, recovery is slow, and sometimes they die.

Temperatures above 30° C (86° F) are also harmful to plant growth. If the roots are exposed to too much heat and dryness or if the new shoots are separated when the roots have been actively absorbing water, the plants will be adversely affected.

Separation of new shoots should be done when the temperature is in the 15° C to 25° C (60–80° F) range. Thus, the most suitable time for separation is May and June, which is the rainy season in Japan. Next best is the middle of September to the beginning of October, which is after the hottest weather.

Although the fall season, September and October, is perfect as far as the temperature is concerned, sometimes special facilities such as a greenhouse may be needed because of the increasing cold. New shoots that are separated in the fall must be well cared for in a warm place.

GREENHOUSE FACILITIES Under normal circumstances, the weather and seasonal conditions dictate decisions about when to separate new shoots from parent kansochiku. However, those with access to a greenhouse may remove the new shoots any time except during midsummer. Greenhouse growers tend to favor December or January in order to give the new plants ample opportunity to recover by the time they are placed outside in April or May. During June, July, and August, the health and vigor of these plants becomes clear, and they quickly develop many new shoots of their own.

EVALUATING NEW SHOOTS Kansochiku usually produce several new shoots every year. Kannonchiku are likely to average two to four shoots, while shurochiku typically produce one or two. There are, of course, some exceptions. For example, one grower reports his experience with a kannonchiku called Shippoden. This particular plant has had as many as nine new shoots at a time, with seventeen in three years. The variety called Zuikonishiki is also known for producing many shoots. A Zuikonishiki may, for example, have four shoots one year, thirteen the next, and five the third year—meaning at least twenty new shoots in three years.

Size of Shoot and Roots   A new shoot may be separated when it has grown at least four or five leaves. Of course, the new shoot must already have its own roots. Usually a few roots come out when the new shoot has three or four leaves; such roots usually have fine root hairs near the ends, which is desirable. However, when a plant has many new shoots, roots might not develop until later. A good rule of thumb is not to separate until there are at least six leafstalks and two roots. One of the roots can be as short as 2 centimeters (1 inch) if the other root is well developed.

When considering whether to separate a new shoot, first count its leaves. Next, remove some soil below the new shoot very carefully with a spatula. If two or more big roots are visible, the plant can be pulled out of the pot. If there are not enough roots, it would be better to delay separating for the time being. The shoots that are not ready to be separated should be left with the original plant and separated later or the next year.

Number of Shoots to Cut   If the original plant has three to five new shoots that are all ready to be separated, do not cut every shoot at once, because it can harm the original plant. It is advisable to leave one or two new shoots and separate them later. This may seem inefficient, but protecting the vigor of the original plant will in the long run result in more new shoots. Also the shoots that are not separated until later will grow better and develop new shoots of their own more quickly.

If shoots are cut off too soon or too many new shoots are removed at one time, they tend to elongate and become disfigured. Therefore, for ornamental purposes too it is recommended that the new shoots be removed at the proper time and that any weakening of the parent plant be avoided.

With a Small New Shoot   The separation should be made when the new shoot has at least five leaves and two strong roots. If, however, an overly small shoot is cut off before it is ready, wind sphagnum moss around the bottom of the shoot. Tie the moss in

Check carefully the number of roots on the new shoot.

A plant ready for separation.

Elongated new shoot has been left with its parent too long.

A too-small shoot is cut by mistake.

Wrap the root well with sphagnum moss.

Plant as usual, with sand and another layer of moss on top.

place with string, and then pot the plant as usual. Frequent use of a vitamin/root-hormone solution is very helpful in minimizing shock and stimulating growth of new roots.

Rejuvenating Old Plants Older kansochiku will eventually cease producing new shoots. Such plants can be rejuvenated either by air-layering (see pages 77–79) or by a simpler method using sphagnum moss. This method rejuvenates simply by placing moss around the bottom of the plant near the soil. Tie it lightly with twine so that watering will not wash away the moss. Keep the moss moist. A new shoot can be expected to come out after a few weeks, in comparison with air-layering, which can take several months and detracts temporarily from the plant's beauty.

PREPARING TO SEPARATE

The Potting Medium Wash river sand thoroughly and sift it using a screen (1.5 millimeter or 1/16-inch mesh) to remove the smaller particles. Next, separate the sand into three grades consisting of large grain (soybean size), medium (pea size), and small (rice size), by sifting the sand through 3- to 4-millimeter (1/8-inch) mesh and 5- to 6-millimeter (1/4-inch) mesh screens.

Always use clean sand. Freshly gathered river sand is ideal. If the sand has been used previously for another plant, be sure to wash it thoroughly to remove any remaining fertilizer or bacteria. Soaking it in a solution of Physan will kill harmful organisms. For shurochiku, add some compost to the small-grain sand. (See pages 56–59.)

Bog or Sphagnum Moss Clean the moss. Remove any rotten portions, and wash the moss with water.

Select the Pot Prepare a pot of the right size for the plant. If the pot is too large, it will retain water too long and will adversely affect the growth of roots. It is better to choose a smaller pot rather than a larger one. (See pages 60–64.)

Check the Roots Kansochiku must be inspected carefully at the base of the new shoots to see whether the roots have grown sufficiently. Remove a small amount of soil in order to check the roots. If the roots are not developed adequately, separation of the new shoots should be postponed. (See page 67.)

How to Separate   Remove the plant from the pot by tapping the rim of the pot.

Before removing the medium from the roots, check the growth of the roots again. If their condition indicates that the new shoots are ready for separation, remove the soil from the roots with a bamboo spatula or a similar tool. If the roots are so tangled that the removal of the soil mix is difficult, put the plant in water and shake it gently to remove the soil. While removing the soil, be very careful not to damage the roots.

When the new shoots and the roots are all exposed, cut off the new shoots from the main body of the plant with a sharp knife or pruning shears.

After severing the new shoots from the parent plant, untangle the roots carefully, and completely separate all parts of the plant.

Cut off any roots that may have darkened due to damage or rotting.

1. Tap the pot's rim to loosen root ball.

2. *Recheck root growth.*

3. *Remove the soil mix.*

6. *The place to cut.*

7. *Cut shoot from parent.*

4. *Wash out any extra soil.*

5. *Gently untangle the roots.*

8. *Carefully separate plants.*

9. *Remove damaged roots before repotting.*

PLANTING THE NEW SHOOTS   Keep the new shoots in water until planting to prevent the roots from becoming dry.

Cover the hole of the pot with a *sana,* to keep the gravel from falling through. A *sana* usually comes with the purchase of a pot. If not, a waterproofed, coarse gauze may be used. The gauze must be a plastic, plastic-coated wire, or stainless steel product. Iron gauze rusts easily and will damage the roots. Although pot fragments are commonly used in place of a *sana,* such a practice should be avoided because the fragments often clog the pot hole, and water drainage and ventilation become inadequate.

After placing the *sana* in the bottom of the pot, add a layer of the largest gravel on top of it. The thickness of this layer should be about 2 centimeters (about 1 inch).

Place a new shoot in the pot with its roots spread and add the medium-grain sand until the pot is about sixty or seventy percent full.

Add the small-grain sand to about the ninety percent level, forming a mound around the plant.

Soak the pot, with the plant in it, in a large bucket of water. Holding the trunk firmly in one hand, gently move the pot in a rotary motion so that the sand will move in among the roots. This agitation in water will settle the potting medium, so add more small-grain sand on top to restore an appropriate level.

Cover the soil well with sphagnum moss. This is essential for preventing both the loss of moisture from the soil and also the loss of soil when watering the plant.

1. Place sana *over drainage hole.*

2. Put large-grained sand in the bottom.

Next add some medium-
~~z~~ed sand.

4. Place plant in pot,
spreading its roots.

5. Add more medium
and then small sand.

Pack the sand with a stick.

7. Immerse in water and twist
to settle sand.

8. Adjust sand level to 90%
of the pot.

Place sphagnum moss
the surface.

10. Properly potted plant.

11. New plant and repotted parent.

Where to Keep Plants   Even the utmost caution may not be able to prevent some amount of damage to the roots during the separation of new shoots. Thus, the plants must be kept away from direct sunlight for the first three weeks afterwards. They may be placed in a warm spot, such as under a table or under a greenhouse bench, to give the plants a rest so that roots can recover from any damage.

In about two weeks, the roots will have recovered to some extent, and the plants can be moved gradually to a spot with more sunlight.

After three weeks, put the plants in a place where they can achieve maximum growth, that is, in a semi-shade area such as under a reed screen or under a tree. Avoid strong direct sunlight.

Watering   Until the roots are well established, it is important to water the newly separated shoots more often than one would water stronger kansochiku plants. However, watering is not needed as long as the soil is moist. Overwatering will keep the soil too damp and will adversely affect the growth of the roots. The point is to keep the soil moist but not saturated.

On days when the soil will dry out rapidly, sprinkling the plants themselves should accompany watering of the soil. This will help them grow better, and any damage to the plants will heal more quickly. Use of misting devices or direct sprinkling on the leaves can cause a buildup of salts, but this disadvantage is of lesser concern when trying to help a newly divided plant recover from the shock of separation. However, sprinkling may burn the leaves of variegated kansochiku, so avoid sprinkling the striped plants, particularly those with many light-colored leaves. Sprinkling should be limited to plain green kansochiku and the more subdued types of striped kansochiku.

Fertilizing   After separation or transplanting, the kansochiku roots are usually damaged. Therefore, immediate application of fertilizer is to be avoided, because it will put further strain on the roots and might even kill the plant itself.

Application of fertilizer should begin one month or more after separation or transplanting. By this time some new roots will have sprouted and will have begun to spread through the soil.

76 Propagation

1. Old elongated plant with few new shoots. ▷

AIR-LAYERING Annual removal of new shoots for transplanting will, after five or six years, cause a kansochiku plant to shed its lower leaves as it grows taller. The aesthetic appeal of the plant gradually declines, and it will eventually cease to produce new shoots. Air-layering is done to rejuvenate such a plant, both to improve its appearance and to encourage it to produce more new shoots.

First, remove the bark of the trunk at an appropriate height, and tie some sphagnum moss around the spot. Normally, the application of moss alone is enough. However, in order to prevent the dehydration of the plant, wrap the moss with plastic sheet in a funnel shape, tying the bottom of it lightly and leaving the top open. Keep the moss moist. Applying a root hormone is helpful.

In a few months, new roots will sprout into the moss. When the roots have grown sufficiently, cut off the top portion of the plant with the new roots, and transplant the top portion into a pot. Ideally, this should be done during the transplanting season of May and June, and because air-layering is a rather slow process the moss should be applied in the very early spring.

After the air-layering, the formerly unsightly plant will be compact and aesthetically pleasing. It will also produce more new shoots.

2. *Cut the bark with scissors.*

3. *Strip off the hairy layer.*

6. *Cover with plastic.*

7. *After many new roots appear, remove moss.*

4. *Wrap the trunk with sphagnum moss.*

5. *Secure the moss with string.*

Cut trunk below roots and plant as usual.

9. *New shoots may form on the old plant after air-layering.*

How to Transplant Kansochiku plants usually produce at least one to three new shoots every year. When the new shoots have grown to adequate size, they should be separated from the parent plant. Thus, the plant will be removed from the pot annually when separating the new shoots and planting them in fresh soil.

Unlike other garden plants, kansochiku plants do not require regular transplanting. The process of separating new shoots to multiply the plants takes the place of transplanting.

However, there are times when transplanting may become necessary. For example, shortly after the separation of new shoots, the plant may grow very rapidly, and the roots may overgrow in the pot, causing poor water drainage and aeration. In such an event, the plant must be transplanted into a larger pot. Also, if a newly purchased plant is in a poor pot or in poor soil, transplanting becomes necessary for healthy growth of the plant.

If, for ornamental purposes, the grower prefers to maintain the plant with multiple trunks, there will be no separation of new shoots and thus no transplanting. However, within a year or two, the roots will overgrow, and drainage and ventilation will deteriorate. As a result, the plant will not grow properly, and it will cease to produce new shoots. If this happens, transplanting is necessary. Usually, a plant that is not divided must be transplanted into a larger pot once in two to three years.

Whether new shoots are separated or not, transplanting may be a necessary maintenance measure. However, as long as the roots have not overgrown, and drainage and ventilation are adequate, transplanting is not required. Even if extreme caution is exercised, transplanting is apt to cause damage to roots and slow down the growth of the plant. Thus, transplanting should be done only when necessary.

The best season for transplanting kansochiku is the same as that for the separation of new shoots, that is, the rainy season of May and June and the period from mid-September to early October. If a greenhouse or a plastic-walled enclosure is available, and hence if the temperature can be maintained constantly above 15° C (60° F), transplanting can be performed any time, except during the high-temperature period in the summer.

The steps to follow in transplanting are almost the same as those for the separation of new shoots. The only difference is that in transplanting the soil that adheres to the roots as the plant is removed from the pot does not need to be completely washed off. In fact, if the soil is entirely removed from the roots, they tend to be damaged.

If the roots are so tangled that the new soil cannot penetrate into that area, the roots should be untangled and the old soil removed. Be careful not to damage the roots. Repotting and maintenance methods are the same as those applied after separating new shoots.

GROWING COMPACT PLANTS   It is possible to produce plants with a particularly dwarfed and compact appearance if special measures are taken. Provide good ventilation, being sure that air movement is adequate and the pots are not crowded together. As time for division of a new shoot approaches, remove the young plant when only five leafstalks are present, rather than the usual six or more. Take fewer roots with the new shoot when it is severed from the parent, even removing if necessary some of the older, larger roots. Use as small a pot as possible for replanting, and provide the plant with stronger light.

KANSOCHIKU BONSAI   When most people think of plants grown on a stone, they think of pine, maple, or *satsuki*, a type of azalea. However, kansochiku plants also provide good material for such "stone bonsai." Smaller, dwarf types such as Kodaruma, Daruma, Himedaruma, or Koban are suitable.

For the stone, a piece of pumice, which absorbs water readily, is ideal. Drill a hole through the pumice large enough to put the kansochiku shoot through it. After removing the soil from the roots, wrap the roots tightly with bog moss and place the kansochiku plant into the hole. No soil other than the moss is necessary. To prevent dehydration, place the bonsai in a low dish or pot with a shallow level of water in it.

8

Daily Care

Kansochiku are subtropical plants, and, characteristic of most members of the palm family, they are by nature very strong. Kansochiku have adapted well to the Japanese climate and are quite tolerant of changes in temperature. Usually the lowest temperature at which kansochiku can grow is about 10° C (50° F), but even when it is around 0° C (32° F) in winter, unless the soil and roots in the pot are frozen, kansochiku will not die. They may stop growing temporarily, but as the temperature begins to increase in spring, the the plants will start to grow again.

Kansochiku are native to subtropical areas, where temperature and humidity are high, but they are found mainly in shaded valleys, where the air circulates and the temperature is relatively low. As a result, the plants are not well adapted to strong sunlight or unusually high humidity. In order to grow kansochiku successfully, the cultivator must place the plants in a suitable environment and care for them with their natural habitat in mind.

CHOOSING A GOOD LOCATION

The fact that kansochiku are adversely affected by too much sun gives some people the erroneous idea that they are essentially weak plants. However, lack of tolerance for full sunlight can be seen as a desirable characteristic when the ornamental uses of the plant are considered. Kansochiku grow well inside houses, under eaves, and under outdoor trees where the sunlight is weak. They can even

Avoiding direct sunlight.

thrive in cities crowded with houses, where plants are deprived of much sunshine. This preference for lower light is in fact a very good feature of kansochiku and is one reason why they are so popular.

Size of the Growing Area For a small number of kansochiku plants, there is no need for a special place or special equipment. During summer, keep them near windows, under eaves, and under trees and shrubs, avoiding full sunlight except in the early morning or late afternoon. If there are no suitable trees or shrubs available, try creating a similar light environment by making a half-shade with a bamboo or reed screen, keeping ventilation adequate so that humidity will not rise too high.

In winter, protection can be provided by bringing the plants inside and placing them on a sunny veranda or in a window location away from cold air. If the temperature is kept constantly above 10° C (50° F), the kansochiku plants will continue to grow well even in winter.

When one's hobby of growing kansochiku becomes more serious and the number of plants increases, some special measures should be taken. It is easiest to water and care for the plants if they are grouped in one place. In winter, there may not be enough space indoors to accommodate all the plants. At this point, the serious

Raindrops can cause the leaves to burn.

grower should consider providing the plants with a special location and acquiring more advanced equipment for their care and propagation.

Rainy Days Frequent rain showers are beneficial to all-green kansochiku varieties. On the other hand, raindrops on the leaves of striped or variegated plants may cause the leaves to burn more easily, and the scars will remain permanently. Therefore, on rainy days it is better to bring the more sensitive variegated plants into the house. If there are too many plants to move, cover them with a plastic sheet or canopy to keep the rain off. Remember that when watering your variegated kansochiku plants it is preferable to avoid wetting the leaves for the same reason. This precaution will also prevent hard water spots from forming on the leaves.

CARE FROM SPRING TO FALL

In spring, kansochiku plants are usually moved outdoors to take advantage of the better growing environment. This can be done by the middle or end of April in warmer regions and by the middle of May in cooler areas.

If the pots are put directly on the ground, they will soon become dirty and splashed with mud. The pots will not look as attractive, and the plants will have poorer ventilation. A plant bench will solve this problem—making daily care easy and displaying the kansochiku to their best advantage.

Lighting Although kansochiku plants do not like much direct sunlight and are healthy under filtered or reduced sunlight, they will not grow well if the light level is too low or if the daylight hours are too short. Under poor light, the plants become weak, the trunk and leaves become unnecessarily elongated and thin, and the production of new plant shoots is reduced.

For good health and propagation, stronger light is desirable, provided the leaves do not get burned. Furthermore, longer daylight results in better growth and multiplication and more attractive plants. Therefore, it is important to choose a sunny place to grow kansochiku. The ideal is to control the sunlight carefully, for example, by using a reed or bamboo screen or shadecloth material.

Morning Sun Exposing kansochiku plants to the softer light of the morning sun is a good way to make them strong and productive. In April, May, and June, expose the plants to direct sunlight until 10 A.M., in July until 9 A.M., and in August until 8 A.M. To better control the morning sunlight, adjust the position of a screen or shadecloth. When the light is weak, the shade can be rolled up completely. In the case of no eastern exposure, when the plants cannot benefit from morning sunlight, the stronger light of afternoon can be controlled by keeping the protective shade in place all summer.

Shading Installation When putting the screen or shadecloth in place, stretch it as high as possible so the light will be well diffused over the plants. The height should be at least one meter (about one yard) above the tops of the plants on the bench. A suitable alternative to reed or bamboo screens and shadecloth is a lath screen that is spaced to filter out about half of the sunlight. If the light is too strong in summer, stretch some shadecloth under the lath screen for additional control.

Ventilation When choosing a suitable growing site, it is also important to consider the need for good air movement. If ventilation is inadequate, the pots may remain wet too long, and the excess moisture in the potting mix will prevent good growth of the roots. Condensed moisture will also remain on the leaves too long, eventually causing the lower leaves to become diseased and drop off. As a result, the plants will become weaker and more susceptible to insect and fungus damage.

Too much air movement is also undesirable. Strong winds can cause the leaves to develop a speckled appearance. Kansochiku pots also dry out very quickly, drying the soil mix and weakening the plants. If the plant bench is on a rooftop or open veranda, close off the growing space from breezes on three sides by constructing wind breaks of reed screens or similar material. Leave the east side open so the kansochiku can receive light from the morning sun.

Winter Care

Kansochiku plants that were grown outside during warm weather should be brought inside in late autumn or as soon as the threat of frost arrives.

For Few Plants   When there are only a few plants, put them on a sunny, warm veranda or on a window sill.

Small Frame House   Another winter possibility is building a small frame house over the plants. Care must be taken, however, because the wide temperature variation from day to night in a frame structure can be harmful to kansochiku. Daytime temperature can exceed 30°C (87° F), and during the night the temperature may be close to 0° C (32° F). It is important to prevent such a large temperature differential. One way is by opening the door to the frame during the warmest daytime hours and covering the frame house at night with straw mats or other insulation to slow the loss of heat. However, these procedures take a good deal of time and trouble. If the plants protected by a frame are not given close attention, they may be damaged fatally. If giving them ideal care is not possible, it is better to bring them indoors, even if the best light is thus sacrificed.

When building a frame structure, make it as large as possible. If it is possible to include such features as double wall covering, good ventilation, and a thermostat, the winter environment will be perfect.

Small Commercial Greenhouse   Small greenhouses for use indoors, on a veranda, or in a corridor are widely available. Many of these are equipped with a thermostat, heater, and ventilator. An added feature of some of these small structures is a lamp, so that sufficient light can be provided for the plants. Ten to twenty pots will fit in the one-square-meter size (about one square yard), and thirty to forty pots can be accommodated in the larger ones.

Using a small commercial greenhouse can save the time required to make a frame structure and will provide a more reliable place to keep the kansochiku in winter. If the light provided in the greenhouse is too low, place it in a sunny corridor or on a veranda. These small manufactured greenhouses are very popular now because plants can be grown indoors, adding to the room decor. For relatively few plants, an indoor-type greenhouse or homemade frame will suffice. However, a collection of many plants will need a real greenhouse or larger frame house.

FOR MANY PLANTS As one's kansochiku plants accumulate, care during the winter months presents more of a challenge. There are several possibilities from which to choose.

Plastic Greenhouses It is simple to build a plastic-covered house, which can be located on any suitable site. Such a structure is especially convenient when the same growing place is used during summer and winter. A plastic house is very easy to construct and to take apart. Not only is it inexpensive but also it will help kansochiku plants grow just as well as will a glass greenhouse.

It is desirable to make the plastic-covered house as big as possible. This helps reduce the change in temperature from daytime to nighttime.

Good ventilation is also very important to keep daytime temperatures from rising to dangerous levels. For this purpose, provide as many large ventilating windows as possible in the top and sides of the greenhouse. A large cooling fan controlled by a thermostat will reduce the need for large window vents.

Rather than completely transparent materials, semitransparent plastic is better for reducing light intensity and retaining heat. The thicker the gauge of the plastic, the more effectively it works. A double covering of plastic, keeping a definite separation between the layers, will provide better insulation against heat loss and better diffusion of sunlight.

Small plastic frame house.

Small indoor greenhouse.

The all-green kansochiku plants and many of the striped cultivars may need no further light reduction than that provided by semi-transparent plastic. Certain of the more sensitive variegated plants will need additional shading to protect their leaves from being burned on the brightest days. Extra shading that can be removed quickly and easily on a dull day is best.

Better Greenhouses Although the cost and time required for construction of a good greenhouse is higher, a real greenhouse lasts much longer than a plastic frame house, and it can be used in all seasons. A well-constructed greenhouse also resists snow and rain much more efficiently and does not require the frequent replacement that is characteristic of low-cost plastic sheets. Some people with building experience might wish to attempt their own greenhouse construction. Others, however, should hire a carpenter or, even better, a professional contractor specializing in greenhouses.

Prefabricated Greenhouses Most prefabricated houses are made in factories in kit form and can be easily assembled using simple tools. Some manufacturers use fiberglass panels, and others use glass. There is no difference in plant growth in either case. The fiberglass-covered house in cheaper, but a glass house lasts longer. Structural material may be all aluminum, which will not rust or rot and requires no paint to preserve the metal frame. Aluminum still costs more than other material, but mass production can keep the cost down.

Prefabricated greenhouses come in various sizes and shapes, to suit a wide range of needs and budgets. Choose the largest greenhouse you can afford. The large space will maintain the temperature stability from night to day. The double glass type provides better insulation but is prohibitively expensive. Attaching a layer of plastic inside the house will accomplish much the same purpose.

A manually adjusted set of top ventilating windows is usually included, but on a warm day temperatures can rise very quickly. At this point, opening side windows becomes essential. For growers who are not at home during the daytime, thermostatically controlled ventilation, although expensive, is very convenient.

In a glass greenhouse, even with an extra plastic layer inside, the strong light will surely burn some of the kansochiku plants. One way to reduce the light is to fasten shadecloth just inside the glass. Another method is to mount lath shading outside above the glass. Both of these measures will help prevent rapid changes in the greenhouse temperature.

HEATING EQUIPMENT Kansochiku plants will not die even if the air temperature drops from 10°C (50° F) to 0° C (32° F), unless the soil in the pots is frozen. They will stop growing at these temperatures, but they will resume growth in the spring. Whether the plants are indoors, on a veranda, in a frame, or in a greenhouse, no more heating is needed to keep the plants alive. Provided the soil does not freeze, they will actually look more compact without any extra heating.

If heating is needed, either to prevent freezing or to keep plants growing, some form of thermostatic control is advisable. At night, a minimum of 15° to 18° C (60–65° F) is best, and during winter days, 20° to 25° C (68–77° F) is adequate. Temperatures that are too high will raise costs and weaken the plants, even though they may be growing well, so keep the heating (and ventilation, if needed) adjusted to avoid temperature extremes.

Leaves are unlikely to be burned in winter because of the reduced light intensity, so the plants may be given plenty of light to strengthen them. Good ventilation is important for growing compact and attractive plants. Even in winter, on mild days when it becomes pleasantly warm in the greenhouse, it is better to open the top vents and side windows enough to provide good fresh-air circulation. Kansochiku plants grow best with about a 10° C (18° F) variation between day and night rather than with perfectly constant temperatures.

In winter, people growing kansochiku plants in a frame, plastic house, or greenhouse often use infrared lamps, a heater, or electrically heated beds or benches to keep their plants growing well. However, the costs of buying and running such equipment are considerable. Rather than increasing heating costs, it is better instead to work on conserving as much of the natural warmth as possible. Cracks and crevices can be covered completely or stuffed with insulation. If possible, install an extra layer of plastic sheeting, or cover a small frame completely with an insulating mat or blanket. Such measures can save all or most of the expense of fuel and equipment, depending on the situation.

Recently many convenient heaters for frames, plastic houses, and

Greenhouse light intensity reduced with reed screens.

Lamps contribute to indoor plant growth.

greenhouses have been developed. An economical heating system can also be made by adapting an existing home heater to one's special situation. Following is a brief description of various heating alternatives, considering their advantages and disadvantages.

Charcoal Using charcoal briquets is a very old method of heating. Being cheap, it is still in use even now. Avoid using charcoal in a closed frame or greenhouse, because during combustion it produces large amounts of carbon monoxide gas (CO) and sulfur dioxide gas (SO_2). Both are very dangerous for people as well as plants.

Remember that growing plants indoors in homes or apartments requires good ventilation to avoid these and other harmful gases. Tight-fitting vent pipes are essential to carry the combustion gases out of the area being heated. Even a small crack can allow gases to reach plants, resulting in toxic symptoms. A charcoal system may be cheap, but an undetected leak can kill all the plants very suddenly, so there is some risk that it will cost more in the long run.

Coal Coal is also relatively low in cost for heating a small- to medium-sized frame or greenhouse. One obvious disadvantage is that it is hard to achieve a constant temperature without continuously feeding in fuel. Coal also produces poisonous gases, so, just as with charcoal, be extremely careful in constructing the chimney.

Gas Natural gas can be used in a special unvented burner designed for use in greenhouses. Synthetic gas, however, should be avoided because of the toxic by-products of combustion.

Propane gas is quite suitable for use in its own special unvented burner, different from a natural gas burner. If carefully designed and adjusted burners are used, both propane and natural gas produce almost nothing but carbon dioxide and water during combustion. These are both good for the growth of plants. However, improperly adjusted natural gas or propane burners give off byproducts that can be very harmful to plants. Be very careful when choosing and controlling such burners. An added hazard of gas or propane burners is the possibility of an explosion.

Kerosene Kerosene is relatively economical and easy to use, but it is very risky because of the possible production of toxic fumes. When installing a kerosene heater that is made to use with plants, be very careful to secure the exhaust duct tightly so there will be no leaks.

Kerosene heaters designed for use in large greenhouses are also available. Others are made to heat steam, which then circulates in pipes throughout the greenhouse. The advantage of using steam heat is that all the combustion can take place outside the greenhouse. However, steam heat requires the expensive installation of piping.

Hot air heaters use large blowers and ducts to distribute the air to different parts of the greenhouse. These are safe because the products of combustion are vented to the outside, and they are economical because the equipment is rather simple. Such systems also achieve uniform temperature throughout the greenhouse because the air is constantly moving.

Electric Heat   The high cost of electricity makes electric heating suitable only for smaller-sized frames, plastic houses, and greenhouses. One good feature of electricity is that it is a clean source of power; any possibility of contaminating the air in the greenhouse is totally avoided. Electric heat is safe and easily controlled automatically, using a thermostat. Installation costs are low and the problems few. Overall, this is the best heating method for a person with a small growing house who wishes to protect a modest number of expensive plants.

For only a few plants, heat can be provided with special poultry-house lamps or, if these can't be found, ordinary light bulbs. First, decide how many bulbs to use according to the wattage and frame-house size. A 60-watt bulb will handle a very small frame, while two or three 1000-watt lamps will be needed for a larger frame. Place the bulbs low because the heat rises. Covering the bulbs with a shield or an empty metal can will prevent them from getting wet and breaking.

Electric Hotbed Wiring   This method uses a special type of resistance wire that is covered with insulation. The shock hazard is removed because of the excellent insulation, and the temperature will not exceed 50° C (122° F), so touching the wire will not burn the skin. Hotbed wire comes in different lengths and wattages and is reasonable in price.

Electric Blower Heaters   A much simpler arrangement than hotbed wires is a specially designed electric heater unit that has a built-in blower. This type of heater is made in various wattages, for either 110-volt or 220-volt outlets. Such a unit is fine for a small- to medium-sized greenhouse but inconvenient without a thermostat.

The Importance of Humidity   Conditions required for good growth of kansochiku plants include adequate light, suitable temperature, and moving air. In addition, because kansochiku plants are native to humid regions, a high level of moisture in the air is a very important requirement. In winter, when the growing space may be heated by various artificial means, the humidity tends to be lowered, resulting in somewhat slower growth. To achieve best growth, some means of adding moisture to the air should be considered.

There are various humidifiers on the market, but many are beyond the hobbyist's budget. One way to substitute for a humidifier is to wet not only the pots but the walkways and areas beneath the plant benches during each watering. When the humidity is quite low, spray the leaves with a misting device that produces a very fine spray.

When a heater of some sort is in use, it may be possible to add moisture to the air by placing a large pan of water on top of the heater. If this is not adequate, spread a layer of pea-sized gravel two or three centimeters (about one inch) thick on top of the plant benches. This layer will hold considerable moisture that can evaporate over a long period. On the other hand, be very careful that the soil in the pots is not constantly wet. Continuous moisture may cause the roots to rot or to grow poorly, and the plants will become weak.

WATERING

It has already been mentioned that river sand with the finest particles removed is ideal for growing kansochiku in pots, because water drains rapidly from such a mixture and the soil dries quickly. But this does not mean that the roots of kansochiku plants prefer to be dry. Rather, they should have moisture always available to at least some parts of the roots. Kansochiku cannot tolerate strong, direct sunlight and must be grown in semishade, so water evaporation is slow. Thus, coarse river sand, which has good drainage and will prevent a waterlogged condition, is the best potting medium for kansochiku.

Their natural habitat being subtropical regions such as Taiwan, kansochiku plants have a natural preference for moisture. These palms are usually found growing naturally near a mountain stream

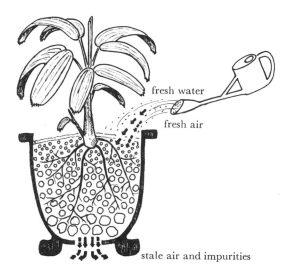

fresh water

fresh air

stale air and impurities

Water until the excess runs out the drain hole.

in the shade of tall trees, where the soil is always moist and where some of the roots are at times exposed to the stream water.

As a general rule, the more the plants are watered, the better the growth of kansochiku will be. However, excessive moisture will make the roots rot, and caution must be exercised not to overwater the plants to the point where roots are soaked constantly. If the pot's drain hole becomes clogged from debris or by the roots themselves, the water sitting in the bottom of the pot will cause the roots to rot.

The danger of overwatering exists not only with kansochiku but with most plants. Plants respire through their roots as well as their leaves. Therefore, if there is too much water in the soil or if water sits in the pot, the respiration function of the roots is impaired, and the roots begin to rot. Furthermore, the stagnant water will be even more harmful if there is fertilizer in the soil, because this causes the roots to rot more quickly.

It is obvious that watering must be done carefully, for roots require not only water but also a proper amount of oxygen. When the kansochiku are planted, the need for good aeration and drainage must be carefully considered. Excess water should drain out quickly, and the roots should have good respiration. To satisfy these considerations, frequent generous sprinkling is the best means of watering kansochiku.

TYPES OF WATER   Any kind of water that is fit for drinking, whether city water or well water, may be used.

City Water   City water usually contains chlorine. Although there is no known proof that chlorine has any adverse effect on plants, as a precautionary measure it is advisable to let the water sit in a bucket for a day before use, so the chlorine can evaporate. During the winter, the temperature of city water is very low, and if used on kansochiku directly the shock of the temperature difference between the water and the soil will damage the roots. During cold seasons, city water should be allowed to stand in a container in the same place where the plants are kept to allow the water to become warmer. The chlorine will escape at the same time.

Well Water   In the winter, well water has a temperature higher than that of the atmosphere and can be given directly to the plant. However, in the summer, well water is colder than the atmospheric temperature and should be allowed to stand for a while until it warms up. If the well water is not being used for drinking, it should be checked by a local health department for any minerals, particularly iron, that might be detrimental to garden plants.

Rain Water   The use of rain water in gardening has been common practice for centuries. However, the recent phenomenon of atmospheric pollution has changed the situation. These days, rain water often contains pollutants and may be harmful to plants.

HOW TO WATER KANSOCHIKU   The purpose of watering is not only to give moisture to the roots but also to circulate the air in the soil. The quantity of water should always be such that a fair amount of water flows out of the pot's drain hole.

If the number of plants to be watered is small, watering may be done simply by submerging the pot in a bucket of water. This method has the advantage of leaching out any excess chemicals that may have accumulated in the soil.

WHEN TO WATER   The time to water can be determined by the extent of drying of the moss covering the soil surface. As long as the moss is moist, watering is not necessary; when the moss begins to whiten due to drying, the plant must be watered. With the exception of striped kansochiku plants, particularly the colorful ones, watering should be done by showering the leaves of the plants from above. This will help the growth of the plants and also lessen the occurrence of diseases and problems with harmful insects. Delicate striped plants should be watered by gently flooding the soil surface, avoiding any water on the leaves.

During the spring and the fall, plants should be watered about once a day; in the summer, about twice a day; and in the winter, once every two or three days. Make minor adjustments depending on the condition of each plant and its potting soil. Water droplets on the leaves may intensify sun rays and burn the leaves, so watering after sundown is preferable.

FERTILIZER

Generally speaking, when growing ornamental plants it is safer to give them too little rather than too much fertilizer. Kansochiku plants can grow sufficiently with very little. However, this means that although the plants can survive, they will have little vitality. They will not produce many new shoots, and hence proper growth and multiplication cannot be expected.

Plants receiving adequate fertilizer have a rich look to their leaves and trunks. Their total appearance is superior, and they have a higher aesthetic value. Such plants also demonstrate good resistance to diseases and insects.

Adequate fertilizer is necessary to the plants' healthy growth and multiplication. In particular, because kansochiku are potted in coarse river sand, they have a lower capacity for holding fertilizer than plants in other kinds of gardening soil. Therefore, kansochiku must be given more fertilizer than other plants would require.

KINDS OF FERTILIZER   There are three basic kinds of commercial fertilizer: the organic type such as a mixture of oil cake, powdered fish, and powdered bone; the inorganic kind such as nitrates, phosphoric acid, and potassium salts; and synthetic fertilizer, which is a combination of various inorganic fertilizing materials. Any one of these may be used with kansochiku. The safest, most effective, and most widely used is the organic kind that is placed on top of the soil in the pot.

Okihi ("place" fertilizer)   This is natural Japanese fertilizer

Commercial fertilizers.

made from oil cake, such as cottonseed meal, as the base, with powdered fish and powdered bone added. The ratio of these ingredients
should be ten to twenty percent each of powdered fish and bone and
the rest made up of oil cake. Mix the ingredients with water to form
a paste. Leave the mixture in a jar for two to three weeks to let it
ferment. Form the material into thumb-sized balls, and allow them
to dry completely. The resulting fertilizer is called *okihi* ("place"
fertilizer). Two or three pieces of *okihi* are placed on top of the soil.

Organic fertilizer is slow acting, but it lasts a long time. At each
watering, a little of the fertilizer dissolves into the soil (its effect is
similar to that of herb medicine). The hard ball of fertilizer prevents
too much from entering the soil at one time, so there is little chance
that the roots will be damaged.

Powdered Fertilizer Another method of fertilizing is to place in
the pot a mixture of oil cake, powdered fish, and powdered bone
(the same mixture as for *okihi* but without adding any water). Although this method is simpler than that for making *okihi*, powdered
fertilizer can be too easily washed away at the time of watering.
Furthermore, powdered fertilizer will ferment in the soil and may

. *Mix well the oil cake, meal, and bone.*

2. Form into thumb-sized balls.

3. Allow to dry completely in the shade.

4. Place 2 or 3 balls of okihi *around the edge every few months.*

damage the roots. Some people put powdered fertilizer under the moss or under the surface of the potting medium to prevent its being washed away, but this should be avoided because the heat generated by the fermentation of the fertilizer may damage the roots.

Liquefied Fertilizer This method starts with fermentation of the oil cake in some water, in a jar kept in the shade. The liquid is then skimmed off and finally diluted with water in a ten-to-one ratio.

Liquefied fertilizer is best used as a supplemental fertilizer, given to the plants once or twice a month. If it is too concentrated, it will cause damage to the roots. To be safe, liquefied fertilizer must be almost as dilute as plain water.

Synthetic Fertilizer Commercially sold synthetic fertilizer comes in various forms: solid (i.e., in grains), powder, and liquid. The chief merit of synthetic fertilizer is the speed of its effect. Some solid kinds combine both slow-acting and fast-acting ingredients. Synthetic fertilizer is easy to use and is not as messy as other kinds.

The grain type of synthetic fertilizer may be used in place of oil cake or powdered fish. Instead of liquefied oil cake, either the powder or the liquid kind of synthetic fertilizer may be used. Application of synthetic fertilizer must be made carefully, with due regard for the amount and the concentration of the solution. Overdosage is one cause of rotting roots. When using synthetic fertilizer, it is better to use half of the amount specified by the maker. In fact, when synthetic fertilizer is used frequently in a dissolved form, make the solution only one-fourth the concentration recommended by the manufacturer. The safe procedure is to use highly diluted solutions often, rather than to give more concentrated solutions less frequently.

APPLYING FERTILIZER Two or three pieces of *okihi* should be applied once every two or three months. In addition, a very dilute liquefied fertilizer should be given as a supplement once or twice a month.

If the temperature of the potting medium decreases to 10° C (50° F) or below, no fertilizing is necessary because the kansochiku become dormant. In fact, application of any fertilizer at this time is harmful to the plant. If the lowest temperature is kept above 10° C, kansochiku will keep growing, and fertilizing must be continued as usual.

Kansochiku plants do most of their growing during the period from May through August. During this time, application of liquefied fertilizer, as a supplemental measure, should be increased to once every ten days, in addition to the regular use of *okihi*. With this program, kansochiku plants will grow rapidly and produce more new shoots.

Fertilizing immediately after transplanting or separation of new shoots must be avoided. Wait at least three weeks after repotting. When the roots have recovered from any damage that might have been caused by transplanting or separation of new shoots, start with *okihi* or some other slow-acting fertilizer.

Disease and Insect Problems

In comparison with other ornamental plants, kansochiku are less susceptible to diseases and insect damage. However, lack of fresh air, infection from other sources, and even minor errors in the planting of kansochiku could at times cause diseases of the plants or damage by noxious insects. The prevention and cure of such adverse effects is an important part of caring for kansochiku.

BROWN SPOT   This is also known as black spot disease, and it is often seen on garden plants with beautiful leaves. When affected by this disease, leaves develop dark brown spots on their surfaces. The spots will spread quickly and will eventually cause shedding of leaves, while weakening the plant itself. This disease has a tendency to affect older leaves more than new leaves; it also occurs more frequently under conditions of high humidity and low temperature. When plants are kept close to each other in the growing area, this fungus disease spreads from plant to plant. When the disease appears on one plant, immediately treat all the plants.

To prevent brown spot, spray the plants regularly at monthly intervals with a preventive chemical fungicide such as Captan, Benlate or Banrot. Once the disease affects the leaves, they retain spots even after they are disinfected, and the plants will lose their aesthetic as well as their monetary value.

ROTTING ROOTS   This is not exactly a disease, as it is caused by

Leaves infected with brown spot.

poor drainage and excessive watering and fertilizing. Lack of experience in maintenance and cultivation and inadequate provision for good aeration also contribute to this problem.

Symptoms of rotting roots include the loss of the plant's vitality, drooping leaves, and a change in the color of leaves at the tips to reddish brown. If any of these symptoms is apparent, remove the plant from the pot and find the cause of the problem. Wash the roots thoroughly with water, remove the rotten root portions, and replant in fresh potting medium.

For best maintenance after replanting, keep the plant in cool shade with good air ventilation in the summer. In the winter, provide it with warm shade. To hasten the recovery of the plant, use a vitamin/root-hormone solution and very little fertilizer.

BURNED LEAVES   This problem, too, is not strictly speaking a disease. Burned leaves occur when there is inadequate shielding from strong, direct sunlight. The colorful striped varieties of kansochiku are particularly susceptible to burning, which can also be caused by sprinkling the leaves with water while they are exposed to strong

Rotting roots cause brown leaf tips.

light. Plants with plain green leaves, if suddenly exposed to strong sunlight after having been grown in the shade, will also be damaged and develop burned leaves.

Plants with rotten roots are also susceptible to burned leaves. The tips of the leaves can be burned to reddish brown. To prevent this problem, provide adequate shielding from direct sunlight and avoid rotting of the roots. Watering the delicate striped kinds of kansochiku must be done with caution. Apply water near the soil surface, taking care to keep the leaves dry. Any exposure to direct sunlight must be done gradually.

INSECTS   Kansochiku plants are affected by very few noxious insects other than scale insects. Unfortunately, these are perhaps the most difficult of all insects to control. Several varieties of scale insect exist; their shells are waxy in texture and have high resistance to penetration of insecticides.

Scale insects infest either side of the leaves, where they suck the sap, weakening the plant itself. The insect multiplies rapidly and spreads to other plants. When plants are infested by scale insects,

Leaf bored by insects before unfurling.

Infestation of scale insects can ruin a plant.

small dots the size of sesame seeds will develop on both sides of leaves, and soon each dot grows larger. At this stage, not only is the plant weakened, but the insect's shell also hardens, making it more difficult to kill. Even if the insects can be successfully removed, scars will remain on the leaves.

Prevention of infestation by insects, early discovery of their presence, and prompt action are the most important controlling techniques. If even the larva of a scale insect is noticed, carefully remove it with a bamboo spatula so as not to damage the leaf, and then spray the plant with insecticide. To prevent infestation by scale insects, spray plants with suitable chemicals once a month. Orthene, malathion, Sevin, diazinon, and Cygon are all effective. After killing the insects with chemicals, remove them carefully with a bamboo spatula in order to reduce damage to the leaves.

9

Outdoor Cultivation

Kansochiku plants may be cultivated not only in a pot as indoor ornamental plants but also as outdoor garden plants. Kansochiku harmonize well with the surroundings in both Japanese- and European-style gardens.

After kansochiku plants were introduced to Japan during the Edo period (1603–1868), they were grown primarily outdoors. Kansochiku were enjoyed mainly as garden plants until pot cultivation methods were developed in the 1920s and 1930s. Even now, kansochiku are frequently found in outside Japanese gardens, although they are cultivated more extensively as container plants.

Because kansochiku plants originated in subtropical regions, places with considerable snow, frost, or cold wind are not suitable for outdoor cultivation. However, with a carefully chosen location and sufficient protection from winter cold, it is possible to grow healthy kansochiku plants in many parts of the world. In relatively warm areas, a shelter to protect the plants from winter snow and frost during the first two years should be enough. After this, the plants should be strong enough to survive the winters with no special protection.

Choosing a Plant

When selecting a kansochiku plant for outdoor use, it is most important to choose one that is healthy, grows actively, and is resistant to cold weather.

Many shurochiku varieties are suitable for outdoor cultivation. Of these, the solid green types, such as Shurochikuao, are the best ornamental plants. They have been used successfully as outdoor plants for many years. Shurochikushima, on the other hand, is sturdy, resistant to cold weather, and very attractive, but it is not suitable for outdoor use because of its high cost and susceptibility to being burned by direct sunlight.

Among the all-green kannonchiku that are strong and healthy, there are many excellent varieties worthy of ornamental use. However, compared with shurochiku, kannonchiku are smaller and less resistant to cold weather, and they grow more slowly. Thus, generally speaking, kannonchiku make a less suitable ornamental outdoor plant than shurochiku. Kannonchiku plants take a long time to grow large after transplanting outdoors, and they tend to look too small for the space allotted.

Choosing a plant for outdoor cultivation should involve the same considerations used when choosing any kansochiku. Do not use new shoots or juvenile specimens as outdoor plants. Instead, choose a good-sized plant with at least three or four shoots. The root system of a young shoot is not well developed and grows slowly, so it needs too much time to grow large enough to become a worthy garden plant. Although suitable plants with several shoots are expensive, they grow vigorously and will be attractive parts of the garden as soon as they are planted.

Choosing a Location

Strong, healthy, and resistant to cold, solid green shurochiku are the most suitable types for outdoor planting. Once they have adjusted to their new environment, these plants become very sturdy and strong, in spite of frost and cold weather. To get the best growth from a plant, it is important to plant it in a location that receives adequate sunlight but no cold wind, especially no north wind.

South or southeast of buildings or fences is the best place to plant. However, any location where there is plenty of sunshine and no strong wind will be suitable. Choose the place to plant after considering the harmony of that location with surrounding buildings or trees. For example, a gate, the side of an entryway, a corner of a veranda, at the foot of a garden stone—any of these may be attractive locations.

The ideal soil is one that permits water to drain rapidly and yet retains considerable moisture. In the case of poorly draining, clay-like soil, generous amounts of river sand and compost should be mixed with the soil to achieve good drainage and aeration. Poorly drained low areas should be avoided as planting sites, if there is a choice. However, it is possible in such a place to build up the soil level and improve its drainage.

OUTDOOR CARE

The most suitable season for planting outdoors is May to June. The middle of September to the middle of October is also appropriate. For outdoor cultivation, the plant should be well recovered from the shock caused by transplanting and should have time to develop an adequate root system before the cold season arrives. The plant will then be better able to pass the winter outdoors. For this reason, the rainy season, from May to June in Japan, is preferable to the fall for outdoor planting.

How to Plant Outdoors   Dig a hole in the ground three times as big as the size of the root ball, and then transplant the plant into the hole, firming the soil lightly around the roots with the foot. Be careful not to lose any of the soil attached to the roots while the plant is being transplanted from the pot to the ground.

After transplanting, water adequately. To ensure that the roots are fully soaked when giving water, direct the water near the center of the plant. During the first two or three weeks after transplanting, protect the plant from too much exposure to the strong, direct sun rays by shielding it with a screen held in place over the plant by a simple frame.

Daily Care   Very little daily care is needed for kansochiku planted outdoors, but after transplanting the plants do need a little attention.

Irrigation   Water occasionally just after transplanting to prevent the soil from becoming too dry. Two or three months after transplanting, the root system will be well established, and watering must be stopped. However, in the summer, when soil tends to become dry, extra water is needed occasionally.

Fertilizers Fertilizing soon after transplanting should be avoided because of the danger of damage to the root system. When the roots are established, about a month after transplanting, apply a mild organic fertilizer such as composted oil meal. A handful of fertilizer should be put in two or three places on the ground 20 or 30 centimeters (8–12 inches) away from the base of the plant, and then the fertilizer should be covered with soil.

Subsequently, fertilizing should be repeated two or three times during the growing period (April to October), at the same interval, using the procedure described above.

Controlling Insects and Disease It is very rare for outdoor plants to be bothered by insects and diseases because plenty of light and good ventilation provide conditions that tend to prevent these problems. However, the plants may occasionally get insects or diseases from some source. As a precaution, during the growing period of April to October, spray with a mixture of fungicide (such as Captan) and insecticide (such as Cygon) at monthly intervals.

WINTER CARE In districts where there are relatively small amounts of snow or frost, during the first year or two after transplanting, some protection should be provided from November until the cold season is past.

Frost damage can easily be avoided by covering the plants with plastic or similar material. The base of the plant should be covered thickly with straw to prevent the soil and roots from freezing. Once the plant is well established and has adjusted to the new environment, the protection during wintertime is no longer needed.

Sometimes the tips of leaves may become somewhat withered because of cold weather or frost. However, this does not cause any serious setback to the growth of kansochiku. When spring comes and the temperature rises, beautiful new leaves will come out again.

Preventing Leaf Damage When a kansochiku leaf is damaged, the disfigurement remains permanently. This spoils not only the appearance of the leaf, but also adversely affects the ornamental value of the entire plant. Therefore, to prevent damage to leaves during wintertime, even in warm districts where there is little frost or snow,

Luxuriant outdoor shurochiku. ▷

use of plastic or some other covering is recommended during extremely cold periods every winter. With such frost protection, the leaves will not be damaged, and there will be very good growth in the spring.

In northern districts and in some highlands of other districts where weather is cold and there is considerable frost and snow, better precautions are necessary. It is important to use rigid plastic on a sturdy frame to prevent its collapse under fallen snow or its being blown off by strong winds.

10

Commercial Aspects

In Japan, kansochiku plants are grown not only for ornamental purposes but also for extra income or as a nursery business. These plants are very suitable for such purposes.

Recently, the demand for potted ornamental plants for indoor decoration has increased sharply along with the increasing number of buildings. To satisfy this demand, new cultivation and production techniques have developed rapidly and are now the basis for modern horticulture.

THE FLUCTUATING PLANT MARKET

Most of Japan's common ornamental plants were introduced after World War II from Europe, the United States, or other countries of origin, mainly in tropical areas. Exotic, attractive, and available in great variety, these tropical plants have been highly valued in Japan for ornamental purposes. Moreover, propagation is easy, and even when special facilities are needed, an amateur can use them to achieve mass production.

However, during the past few years, there have been some signs of confusion in the marketing of such ornamental plants. Changes in the market prices have become exaggerated, and over-production has resulted in dropping prices. These changes have menaced producers and caused great anxiety.

These changes have been occurring for two main reasons: over-production and decreased demand. In Japan, the government has been encouraging cuts in rice production, so farmers have been turning to cultivation of ornamental plants to subsidize their incomes. Consumer demand, on the other hand, has not always risen with production. The delicacy of tropical plants, and their low resistance to cold have tended to discourage many plant owners. While their use in offices and restaurants remains common, decorative tropical plants are found less and less in the Japanese home.

In contrast with the depressed market for European ornamental plants, native Japanese plants and others that have been in Japan for centuries are enjoying renewed popularity. These include Oriental orchids, flowering trees like azaleas, Japanese alpine plants, bonsai, and kansochiku. The latter, in particular, have shown striking development in recent years, based on their attractive appearance, easy propagation, and strength. The market price of kansochiku has been continually stable from the time when colorful, tropical ornamental plants were at the height of their popularity through the present. The demand for kansochiku has been increasing, in spite of the recent reduced interest in Japan in most ornamental plants. Thus kansochiku plants are unique in maintaining stable market prices during recent years.

Recently, the rise in demand for kansochiku plants has been greater than the increase in supply, so kansochiku have a high market value. Since both the supply and the demand can be expected to continue increasing steadily, commercial growing of kansochiku, as either a full-time or a supplemental business, is very promising and can provide stable benefits.

ADVANTAGES OF KANSOCHIKU

Kansochiku are ideal plants for commercial production, for many reasons.

1. Variety Is Abundant and Everchanging. There are many varieties of kansochiku plants, and these are continually changing. Abundance of variety encourages people to collect many different types of kansochiku to satisfy various demands and tastes. As a result, their appeal remains undiminished.

About half of the kansochiku varieties belong to the striped and patterned categories. Even within the same variety of plant, each specimen shows different patterns or characteristics. Certainly there are no two striped plants that are exactly the same. Therefore, even when collecting and cultivating the same variety, kansochiku plants with varying patterns can be grown. Kansochiku enthusiasts are always eager to acquire different varieties and additional specimens of the same variety, as far as money and space permit—a favorable consideration for kansochiku producers.

2. Make Money While Enjoying the Plants.   Many people growing kansochiku find that the number of plants increases spontaneously, resulting in large profits. Kansochiku can be an enjoyable hobby and, at the same time, a profitable business.

3. Large Investment Unnecessary.   Because the price of a pot of kansochiku is higher than that of other ornamental plants, people think a big investment must be made when starting this business. However, this is not necessarily so. Needless to say, to make a lot of money in a short time, the investment will have to be large in order to correspond to the profits sought. However, with a long-term plan, commercial cultivation can begin with a small investment. Later it is possible to expand to large-scale growing or commercial production of expensive medium- or high-class varieties.

Kansochiku plants produce one to three new shoots each year. At the least, one plant will increase to two or more plants. This means that the number of plants doubles every year. Thus, one pot of kansochiku will become two pots a year later, and four and eight pots two and three years later, respectively. After ten years, there will be over a thousand pots. Even a conservative estimate of half this amount demonstrates the very high chances of success with kansochiku.

Do not be discouraged when starting with a small investment and only a few plants. As the plants increase in number year by year, the grower's skill improves. For this reason, a gradual investment is in fact the best route for a beginner. When the number of pots becomes too large, and there is not enough space or equipment to care for them, sell some of the plants and buy kansochiku of a higher grade. This procedure will insure more benefits with limited space and a smaller investment.

4. Ease of Care and Simple Equipment.   Although kansochiku were originally tropical plants, they have become environmentally adapted to the climate in Japan and other temperate-zone locations such as the United States and Europe. They exhibit high resistance to damage by insects and disease. They are very strong plants and easy to propagate. These are advantages not only for amateur growers but also for commercial cultivators. In mass production, care is very easy, and no skillful techniques or labor are required. Even beginners, with only a little basic instruction, can achieve good results.

In contrast with other ornamental plants, no conventional greenhouse and heating apparatus is necessary for kansochiku cultivation. The plants can remain outdoors in summertime and in a simple plastic-covered house in wintertime. If there is no objection to the plants becoming dormant in winter, heating is unnecessary, but be careful not to allow the roots or soil in the pots to freeze. With only modest precautions, the plants can pass the winter without any problem. During extremely cold periods in winter, use of a simple heater will prevent a serious drop of temperature. It is actually better for kansochiku to receive no regular heating in wintertime, because heating tends to cause abnormal elongation, loss of the plants' attractive compact shape, and thus reduction of their value.

Expenses for kansochiku equipment and fuel are relatively low, keeping their cultivation economical, a consideration of particular importance to the commercial grower.

5. Mass Cultivation in a Small Space. Large areas are not required for growing kansochiku plants, and even with a small space mass cultivation and high profits are possible. For example, with big pots (18 centimeters, or 7 inches, in diameter), fifty pots can easily fit into an area of about 3 square meters (approximately 3 square yards); in about 70 square meters, 1,000 pots can be accommodated. Even when different growing locations in summer and winter are used, a total of about 130 square meters should be sufficient for commercial cultivation.

Let us consider an example. A person growing the cheapest popular all-green varieties, such as Daruma, Koban, Fukuju, Kodaruma, and Tenzan, can make more than 1,000 yen (about $5) profit per pot in one year. A thousand pots will produce a million yen (about $5,000). An area of 330 square meters can support 2,500 to 3,000 pots, resulting in a potential yield of 2.5 to 3 million yen. Even if 20 percent of the earnings is budgeted for

Lath and plastic screening can protect many plants at once. ▷

pots, fertilizer, and fuel, raising kansochiku can yield high profits compared with growing other ornamental plants. One person can easily manage a space of 330 square meters and about 3,000 pots, even on a part-time basis.

6. Stable Market Price. Kansochiku cannot be propagated by ordinary methods of grafting or rooting cuttings. The only suitable method of multiplication is to separate the new shoots. For this reason, it is impossible to mass-produce kansochiku. A sudden drop in price, as observed in other ornamental plants, is thus very unlikely in the case of kansochiku, and the market price remains stable. In fact, the demand for kansochiku has been greater than the supply for many years.

7. Sell in All Seasons. Kansochiku are in demand in all seasons, because they look lovely and make fine gifts year-round. Because they are so strong, kansochiku suffer very little damage while being displayed in a shop, and they will not wither just after purchase. Even if some plants remain unsold, they will gradually grow and produce new plants, actually benefiting the seller.

8. Demand is High. Kansochiku are sold mainly to gardening fans who cultivate and enjoy the plants. In addition, they are sold as ornamental plants for decoration. Inexpensive and popular kansochiku varieties are always sought after, so the grower need not be concerned about shrinking demand.

PROFITABLE GROWING METHODS

There are three methods of cultivating kansochiku for a part-time or full-time business: 1. mass cultivation of inexpensive and popular varieties; 2. cultivation of popular varieties as main products and of middle-grade and high-grade varieties as minor products; 3. cultivation of middle-grade and high-grade varieties only.

Method 1 All-green varieties, being strong and having a high rate of multiplication, are a good example of a cheap and popular type of kansochiku plant. Because the price of all-green kansochiku is low, there is a large demand and little change in the market price. Cultivation of all-green varieties is recommended to people who have a relatively large land area or to beginners who have little experience but intend to start commercial cultivation.

Varieties Suitable for Growth in Large Numbers

Kodaruma · Hakkokinshi · Himedaruma · Kinshi · Mangetsu
Daifukuden · Daruma · Namikannonchiku · Daikokuten · Tenzan
Shurochikuao · Shippoden · Koban · Kodaruma · Heiwaden
Keigetsu · Taiheiden · Aikokuden · Fukuju · Chiyodazuru

Varieties Suitable for Small-Space Growing

Middle Grade

Hinodenishiki · Kannonchikushima · Zuikonishiki · Shurochikushima
Kinsho · Toyonishiki · Towaden · Kobannishiki · Kotobuki

High Grade

Tokainishiki · Tenzanshiroshima · Nanzannishiki · Tenzannoshima
Eizannishiki · Darumanoshima · Shirotaenishiki

Method 2 This method is recommended for those with only a small growing area, who cannot expect high enough profit by cultivating only popular varieties. It is also suitable for people who want to make more profit than the first method can produce.

This method stresses popular all-green kansochiku varieties to provide a stable basis for profit. In addition to this type, some striped and patterned kinds, which are middle- or high-grade kansochiku, are grown. Although these more expensive plants multiply slowly, high profits can be gained from small numbers of plants. This is the most desirable method in commercial cultivation of kansochiku, combining a small land area and high profits.

Method 3 This method requires the least land and can give the highest profits. Care of the more expensive plants is not difficult. However, it is very risky for beginners to adopt this method, for a big investment is required. Small numbers of pots can give high profits, but all varieties are not in equal demand. Even within the same variety, big differences in profits result from the varying nature of individual plants. Generally speaking, whether a plant gives profits or not depends upon the nature of each plant. The ability to distinguish the quality of each plant can be acquired only from long experience in growing kansochiku and not from being taught by someone else.

CHOOSING AMONG THE METHODS   The market for the middle- and high-grade varieties is limited because of their higher prices, so skillful sales are required. There is no profit if the plants cannot be sold, and it is difficult for a beginner to acquire good sales ability. Proper guidance from an experienced grower or plant trader can solve this problem, but without such assistance, it may be best to begin with Method 1.

The beginner who does adopt Method 3 should first obtain experience in cultivation and master the techniques by growing popular varieties that have high rates of multiplication. After gradually acquiring the ability to judge and select good plants, as well as mastering growing techniques and sales methods, then it is safe to start growing middle- and high-grade products.

Today, Method 3 is in wide use in Japan for the commercial growing of kansochiku plants. A small land area and one's own labor can result in high profits, an approach consistent with the high cost of land and residential housing in Japan. There are many examples of people developing the cultivation of kansochiku plants as simply a hobby, only to find that the number of their plants increases spontaneously, resulting in big profits.

SELECTING PLANTS

For commercial cultivation, it is very important that the beginner decide which varieties to acquire and know which varieties can return the highest profits. However, in growing kansochiku plants, it is even more important for both beginners and experienced persons to decide how to cultivate each variety than to decide which variety to select.

Needless to say, selection of variety should not be neglected. Popularity of the plant depends upon the variety, and some varieties are easier to sell than others. Some varieties are also easier to grow and have higher rates of multiplication than others.

The general rule of thumb should be to produce the finest possible plants; these will have the highest commercial value. High quality plants of any variety will bring high prices.

A beginner just starting to grow plants for sale should ask an experienced person or dealer to suggest varieties best suited for commercial cultivation. Grow mainly these plant varieties, mastering the cultivation techniques and learning the characteristics of each variety. It will gradually become apparent which varieties are most suitable for any particular growing conditions. From then on, concentrate on these varieties.

It is better to raise only varieties having the same characteristics and avoid special types with diverse requirements that may not be easily met. This approach means easier care for the plants and a higher likelihood of good plant growth, resulting in plants of higher value. From the standpoint of sales, a single product is easier to manage and can be sold at a higher price compared with a multitude of products.

SUITABLE VARIETIES   When selecting varieties of kansochiku plants for the first time, choose those varieties that tend to produce many new shoots and that have an attractive shape. Kansochiku varieties with such properties are listed in the table on page 117. Of these, Daruma, Koban, Kodaruma, Tenzan, and Shurochikuao have been used most frequently for commercial cultivation. These are common and popular kansochiku varieties, indicating that they have high multiplicity, good growth rates, and high ornamental value. The demand for them is steady, and hence they are easy to sell.

At first, grow only those varieties that are strong and easy to care for, have a high rate of multiplication, and are easy to sell. When the entire growing space is filled with plants, concentrate on the best-growing varieties. After gaining experience, then try growing middle- and high-grade variegated plants in order to achieve more profits.

When choosing more desirable and expensive striped and spotted varieties, adopt the same procedure. At first, select more popular varieties that have high multiplicity, strength, beauty, high ornamental value, and easy sales potential. Concentrating on such varieties makes the best use of growing facilities and will maximize profits. Then, by reinvesting profits, try growing additional varieties.

SELECTION OF ORIGINAL PLANTS The procedure for selecting the parent kansochiku plants for commercial growing is the same as that already described in the general section on selection (pages 49–53). For commercial cultivation, select the first plants very carefully, because these original plants are the key to good multiplicity and high profits. Avoid baby plants or old ones from which many young plants have already been obtained. It is best to select young and healthy plants, even though they are more expensive.

In the case of striped and spotted kinds of middle- and high-grade kansochiku, the selection of the original plants is especially important, because the quality of the parent will have a big effect on profits. The procedure for selecting original variegated plants is the same as that described previously (pages 52–53). The most important thing is to get the very best plants possible, even though they are more expensive.

There are two methods for purchasing the original parent plants. One is to buy them directly from dealers, growers, retail outlets, or hobbyists. The other method is to choose a particular dealer and producer and buy everything through that one person. For the novice in commercial growing, the latter method can be recommended. The dealer can be very helpful in giving advice on cultivation and choosing the original plants. Arrange to sell your plants through this same dealer. In this circumstance, the dealer not only will select good original plants but also can be helpful in selling your products—a very convenient arrangement for the beginner. Moreover, the dealer often can sell the plants at higher prices than an amateur could.

HOW TO GROW COMMERCIALLY

In commercial cultivation of kansochiku plants, the methods of selection and purchase of varieties or particular plants, as described earlier, and the methods for selling the plants produced, which will be discussed later, are important factors. However, a more important consideration is how to care for these beautiful plants so that they will have high commercial value. To achieve the highest quality, it is vital to pay attention to all details of cultivation techniques and daily care of the plants, which have been discussed at length in Chapter 8.

In Summary

1. Keep the growing space well ventilated: cool in summer and warm, if possible, in winter.

2. Light is necessary for the plant to achieve good growth and multiplication. Let the plant receive sunlight for as long as possible each day, but reduce the light's intensity to avoid burning the plant leaves.

3. Space the plants so there is a suitable distance between pots. Otherwise, the ventilation will be poor. Crowded plants may have shortened lives, and disease or insects will develop more easily. An abnormal elongation of the leafstalks may also result from crowding the plants too closely.

4. When transplanting kansochiku plants, use sufficiently coarse sand to achieve good drainage, and then water adequately.

In the case of all-green kansochiku, watering the leaves produces good growth. However, with variegated kansochiku plants, especially when the light-colored stripes are dominant, watering the leaves should be avoided because they may be burned.

Even among all-green plants, if the leaves are watered at a time of day when the plant is receiving direct sunlight, a drop of water can work as a lens, and the leaf may be burned. Therefore, watering during the daytime may be dangerous for the plant. Frequent watering of the leaves also can result in unsightly hard-water deposits.

5. In fertilizing there is a knack to achieving good growth and handsome plants without applying too much fertilizer. When applying *okihi* fertilizer, use composted oil meal and replace it every month or two in order to keep the fertilizer on the surface of the pot soil. During the active growing period for plants, from spring through summer, give additional fertilizers, such as a dilute solution of fermented oil meal or a solution of Hyponex, two or three times per month. A concentration of about 200 ppm for all-green plants and about 100 ppm for variegated plants is about right. (One gram of 20–20–20 soluble fertilizer added to one liter of water gives a concentration of 200 ppm of N, P, and K. The same

proportions can be achieved by adding one ounce of this fertilizer to $7\frac{1}{2}$ gallons of water.)

6. The control of diseases and insects is one of the most important measures needed to produce beautiful, valuable plants. Suitable fungicides and insecticides should be sprayed on the plants once or twice each month.

7. During the wintertime keep the plants in a greenhouse or a plastic frame house. If no growth is desired during the wintertime, it is not necessary to use a heater, except in extremely cold places. Keeping the temperature of the growing area at least 15° C (60° F) allows the plant to continue growing and produce new shoots even in wintertime.

On the other hand, too high temperatures result in an abnormal elongation of the plant, so avoid keeping the plants too warm. Even with no heating in winter, daytime temperatures in a greenhouse or a plastic-covered house rise very high. As a result, the plants may be damaged or have their growth inhibited by the extreme temperature difference between day and night. It is important to open the top and side windows in the greenhouse during the daytime on a hot day to provide ventilation and to prevent a sharp rise of temperature in the room.

8. Shurochiku can be planted outdoors for commercial cultivation because of their high resistance to cold weather. Much of the time and work of watering the plants can be saved this way. During wintertime, simple facilities for preventing frost damage, like a plastic covering, will keep the plants healthy throughout the cold season. However, much work is needed to dig them up and establish them in containers before they can be sold.

9. For those wishing to use a potting mix that needs less frequent watering than potting sand, a very loose, coarse artificial soil mix, such as that used for African violets, should work well. With such a mix, watering once a week in warm weather may be adequate if humidity is high.

MARKETING KANSOCHIKU

In the commercial growing of any kinds of plants, production methods are the most important consideration. Second only to this is successful sales. There are several methods for marketing kansochiku plants.

1. Selling to customers at a nursery or store run by the grower. Since the number of people who enjoy kansochiku plants is rapidly increasing, this method can be very successful. However, there is some risk, because of the limits on time and the number of customers. Furthermore, it may be difficult to sell off varieties that have accumulated in large numbers.

2. Selling to wholesale dealers or to gardening stores and nurseries. This is the easiest and soundest way, although it results in prices slightly lower than those to be gained from selling directly to customers. However, with handsome and valuable plants, the market demand is always higher than the supply, so it is possible to sell continually and still make money.

3. Selling at swap meets or plant auctions. In Japan, monthly swap meets and auctions are held on designated days in certain districts and sponsored by dealers or hobbyists. Anybody can attend and bring plants for sale.

4. Shipping plants to special kansochiku markets. This method is not suitable for middle- or high-grade plants, but it is fine for selling a large quantity of lower-priced, popular kansochiku. There is a strong demand for kansochiku plants in any ornamental plant market. Kansochiku can be sold in large quantities throughout the four seasons.

DEMAND FOR PLANTS WITH HIGH ORNAMENTAL VALUE   There is a big difference in demand among the plant varieties, depending on the nature of individual plants. Even in the same variety, a compact and beautiful plant will bring a higher price than a poorer specimen. The plant with leaves that have bruises or show damage from insects or diseases due to poor cultivation techniques, or with abnormally elongated leafstalks, will have a low commercial value. It is thus essential for commercial purposes to raise healthy and beautiful plants. Always strive for improvement in cultivation techniques and in daily care of the plants.

11

Seasonal Care

SPRING: MARCH TO MAY

As the weather gets warmer, the kansochiku growing season begins. Plants that have been kept indoors or in a plant frame for winter protection are now taken outdoors when the danger of frost has passed. In regions of Japan with warmer weather, this may be about the end of April. In less favored areas, wait until the middle of May.

It is not good for plants to be kept indoors more than is necessary, particularly if ventilation is inadequate. If plants are kept indoors too long under poor conditions, they may become weak and less attractive, and their ability to produce new shoots may decline.

When moving plants outside, choose a spot that is sunny and has plenty of moving air. But be careful to protect the plants, especially at first, from too much light and wind. This can be done with bamboo screens or shadecloth.

Be very cautious to avoid changing the environment of plants too suddenly, for plants can be damaged by markedly different conditions. When ready to begin moving the plants, alter their environment gradually by opening a window during the day. Each day, increase the length of time the window is left open. Begin by exposing the plants to a little morning light, but be careful to avoid burning. Softer morning light starts the plants growing safely.

As the plants are strengthened before they are taken outdoors, watering must be checked more closely to avoid the roots' getting too dry. Water every day or two as needed. After the plants are outdoors, watering must be done daily. If the weather is unusually dry and windy, it may be necessary to water twice a day.

Fertilizing should begin soon after the plants have been moved outside. Diluted complete soluble liquid fertilizer, such as Hyponex, will be needed about once or twice each month.

There is very little danger from insects while the kansochiku are growing in the protected indoor environment. However, when they are growing rapidly outdoors, they are subject to insect damage. Insecticides should be used at least once a month for protection.

About the middle of May is a good time to repot the plants. This is needed when excessive root growth interferes with passage of water through the root ball. If the indoor temperature is seldom below about 15° C (60° F), repotting can be done before mid-May. Under these favorable conditions, the plants will already have recovered from the shock of dividing and transplanting by the time they are moved outdoors.

The middle of May is also a good time of year to plant kansochiku outdoors in the ground. This is particularly true for shurochiku, which are better adapted than kannonchiku to cold weather when planted in the garden.

Summer: June to August

June is the rainy season in Japan, and kansochiku plants can be seen making new growth almost daily during such favorable weather. After the rainy season, the sunlight is at maximum strength, so be very careful not to let the leaves get burned. During the rainy season it is best not to allow the variegated plants to receive water directly on their leaves because there is risk of damage. Keep them indoors or under shelter. Also, when watering variegated plants, it is generally preferable to avoid wetting the leaves, although some growers have begun to think that keeping water off the leaves is not as important as it was once considered to be.

Summer is the hottest season and thus the best for rapid plant growth. Because of the heat it is very easy for plants to become too dry at their roots as well as too low in humidity for the leaves. Water more frequently than is usual in other seasons. Normally water will be needed once in the morning and once in the evening during the hottest weather. During unusually hot, dry weather, inspect the moss covering the soil, and water more frequently than twice daily if it has become too dry.

Because plants grow most actively during summer, their need for fertilizer is greatest. Put on new *okihi* fertilizer and also give them Hyponex or other soluble or liquid fertilizer once or twice each month. If any plants that had been divided earlier are now well established, start fertilizing them.

Summer is a time to watch closely for insects; spray with insecticide solution once or twice a month. Be very careful to avoid a buildup of such pests on your plants.

The middle of June is a very good time to divide any plants that were not ready for separation earlier. It is also best to plant before mid-June any kansochiku that are to go into the ground.

Autumn: September to November

Kansochiku plants stop growing for a while when the weather is too hot in midsummer. After September, as cooler weather approaches, growth once more becomes good. Because the sunlight is still fairly intense, be careful to avoid burning the leaves. Autumn is typhoon season in Japan, and the strong winds can be very damaging to the leaves of the plants. Protect them from anticipated strong winds by moving them to a more sheltered area.

About the end of October frosts begin. Because kansochiku plants are quite sensitive to frost, move them indoors or to a plant house for protection from cold. Shurochiku growing in the ground should be covered with a special insulating plastic when frost or snow is expected. This is particularly necessary in colder climates. Also some insulation of the root area to prevent freezing may sometimes be needed.

The first part of September may still be quite hot, so watch very carefully to be certain the plants don't get too dry. Watering twice a day may still be necessary until cooler weather arrives.

The fall season allows the plants to recover from the strain of hot summer weather and gets them ready for the cold ahead. Be sure to give them enough new fertilizer to replace the amounts lost by frequent watering during hot weather. Continue to give supplemental feedings of dilute fertilizer solution once or twice a month, if cool weather has not yet arrived.

As cooler weather begins, the rate of growth decreases, and the use of fertilizer should be reduced accordingly. The beginning of autumn is also a time to be on guard against insect infestation. At least once or twice a month, use suitable insecticides as a preventive measure. As temperatures decrease, so will the activity of insects, but continue to use insect sprays at least once a month until the coldest weather arrives.

Division of young plants from the parent plant, followed by repotting, can be done from about mid-September to mid-October. This same time period is also quite suitable for planting kansochiku directly in the ground.

WINTER: DECEMBER TO FEBRUARY

Plants that are moved into a house or greenhouse may be kept at lower temperatures if growth during the cold period is not desired. Even if the temperature should fall to freezing, plants that have been moved indoors will be safe, for they are strong and able to tolerate cold weather. Of course, it is necessary to acclimate the plants gradually to such low temperatures.

If the room is kept above 10°C (50°F), kansochiku will continue growing slowly. Very little cost is involved in heating the plant space to the 10–15°C (50–60°F) range. If the temperature is kept too high, the plants will survive, but they may lose their most attractive compact form. Too high temperatures may also weaken the plants to some extent, lowering their quality. Even if speedy plant growth in winter is attempted by heating, it is best to rest them for a few weeks at lower temperature and then gradually begin heating. If the plants are kept in a greenhouse, try to avoid large differences in day and night temperatures during winter. Sunny winter days are a problem in a greenhouse, for very high temperatures can easily result. Good ventilation helps to keep temperatures down. A little change in temperature from night to day is good and will produce plants of better quality. The use of insulating mats at night to cover the plants helps keep the temperature from dropping too rapidly.

It is important to give the plants enough sunlight in winter. Winter sunlight is usually low enough in intensity that there is little danger of burning the leaves. Plants receiving enough sunlight will grow much better when spring arrives.

Watering once every two or three days in cool temperatures is often sufficient. But plants in a warm environment may still require daily watering. Check frequently to be sure that the moss on the soil surface has not dried out.

Fertilizer is not needed when temperatures stay below 10°C (50°F). If the temperature in the house or greenhouse is above 10°C (50°F), the slow but continued growth of the plants requires a little fertilizer. One new *okihi* fertilizer ball in winter plus dilute liquid fertilizer solution once or twice a month is about right.

It is very unlikely that insect problems will develop if the plant growing space is not heated in winter. One or two preventive spray treatments for the entire winter should be adequate. If higher temperatures are provided, it is very easy for insects to multiply. In this case it will be necessary to spray for insects once or twice each month.

If temperatures are kept at 15°C (60°F) or above in winter, the plants will grow so much that dividing and repotting them may be necessary.

Plants growing in the ground outdoors in colder areas will need to be covered during the winter with plastic. Straw mats or other insulation may be needed around the root area to prevent freezing.

Appendices

1. KANSOCHIKU REGISTRATION

The first kansochiku registration list as issued by the Kansokai (Japan Kansochiku Association) in 1940. It included 35 varieties, most of them solid green types that had long been popular in Japan. Since then, additions have been made almost annually.

DATE	NAME
1942	Hinodenishiki
1949	Choyo, Taiheiden, Uchuden
1951	Asahinishiki, Hakumeijo
1952	Kotobuki
1953	Daifukuden, Heiwaden, Shoryu
1954	Kotobuki
1955	Hakuseiden, Mangetsu
1957	Aikokuden, Meisei, Tenmanishiki
1958	Tokainishiki
1959	Hakuju, Zuishonishiki
1960	Darumanoshima
1962	Shirotaenishiki
1963	Darumanozu, Fukiden, Hakuhonishiki, Kinkonishiki, Otohime, Shippoden
1964	Kinsei, Fukuryu
1965	Hagoromonozu, Keigetsu, Tenzannoshima
1966	Chiyodazuru, Nikkoden, Ogonmaru, Shihonoshima, Tenryu
1967	Kobannishiki, Tenzanshiroshima
1970	Mangetsunozu, Nanzannishiki, Toyonishiki
1971	Choju, Kodarumanishiki, Towaden
1972	Daikokutennoshima, Koganenishiki, Tenshi
1973	Eizannishiki, Daikokunishiki
1974	Mangetsunoshima, Showanishiki, Shozannishiki
1975	Kodarumanoshima
1976	Ayanishiki, Hakutsurunishiki
1979	Aikokudennoshima, Keigetsunoshima
1980	Fukujunishiki
1981	Horainishiki, Shiroganenishiki

129

	Optimal Growing Conditions			Leaf	Ch
	Percentage of Shade	Concentration of Fertilizer	Temperature	Leaf Size	No. Leaf
Sᴛʀɪᴘᴇᴅ Kᴀɴɴᴏɴ-ᴄʜɪᴋᴜ					
Ayanishiki	55	medium	18 °C (64 °F)	medium	2–
Chiyodazuru	55	weaker	20 °C (68 °F)	medium	2–
Choju	60	medium	20 °C (68 °F)	medium	2–
Daikokunishiki	60	medium	23 °C (73 °F)	medium	3–
Daikokutennoshima	60	medium	23 °C (73 °F)	medium	2–
Darumanoshima	60	medium	20 °C (68 °F)	medium	5–
Eizannishiki	60	weaker	20 °C (68 °F)	medium	2–
Hakuju	65	medium	20 °C (68 °F)	medium	2–
Hakutsurunishiki	60	weaker	20 °C (68 °F)	medium	2–
Hinodenishiki	60	medium	23 °C (73 °F)	medium	2–
Kannonchikushima	65	medium	20 °C (68 °F)	medium	2–
Kinkonishiki	60	medium	20 °C (68 °F)	large	3–
Kobannishiki	65	weaker	20 °C (68 °F)	small	2–
Kodarumanishiki	60	weaker	20 °C (68 °F)	small	2–
Kotobuki	65	medium	20 °C (68 °F)	medium	2–
Nanzannishiki	50	stronger	23 °C (73 °F)	medium	2–
Shirotaenishiki	65	medium	23 °C (73 °F)	large	3–
Showanishiki	65	medium	20 °C (68 °F)	medium	2–
Tenmannishiki	60	medium	23 °C (73 °F)	large	3–
Tenzannoshima	60	medium	20 °C (68 °F)	large	2–
Tenzanshiroshima	60	medium	20 °C (68 °F)	medium	2–
Tokainishiki	60	medium	25 °C (77 °F)	medium	2–
Toyonishiki	50	medium	23 °C (73 °F)	medium	2–
Uchuden	60	weaker	20 °C (68 °F)	small	2–
Zuikonishiki	50	medium	20 °C (68 °F)	medium	2–

Leaf ickness	From Average Quality Parents			From Choice Quality Parents		
	Percentage of Choice Shoots	Percentage of Average Shoots	Percentage of Poor Shoots	Percentage of Choice Shoots	Percentage of Average Shoots	Percentage of Poor Shoots
n	80	15	5	90	5	5
n	80	15	5	100	...	...
n	20	30	50	35	35	30
ck	15	25	60	30	35	35
ck	15	30	55	35	35	30
dium	20	30	50	35	35	30
dium	25	25	50	75	15	10
n	15	30	55	35	30	35
n	20	35	45	35	35	30
ck	20	35	45	35	35	30
n	20	35	45	35	35	30
ck	15	25	60	35	30	35
ck	80	15	5	100	...	...
dium	15	25	60	35	35	30
n	20	35	45	40	30	30
ck	25	25	50	70	20	10
ck	15	25	60	30	35	35
dium	20	35	45	35	35	30
ck	20	25	55	35	35	30
dium	25	25	50	40	35	25
dium	25	25	50	40	30	30
ck	25	30	45	45	30	25
ck	35	40	25	65	20	15
in	100	...	...	100	...	...
in	40	35	25	70	20	10

	Optimal Growing Conditions			Leaf Cha	
	Percentage of Shade	Concentration of Fertilizer	Temperature	Leaf Size	No. Lea
SOLID GREEN KANNONCHIKU					
Aikokuden	55	medium	23 °C (73 °F)	medium	2–
Daikokuten	50	medium	23 °C (73 °F)	medium	3–
Daruma	50	stronger	20 °C (68 °F)	medium	5–
Fukuju	50	medium	20 °C (68 °F)	medium	2–
Heiwaden	55	medium	23 °C (73 °F)	large	1–
Koban	50	medium	20 °C (68 °F)	small	1–
Kodaruma	50	stronger	20 °C (68 °F)	small	2–
Mangetsu	50	medium	23 °C (73 °F)	medium	2–
Namikannonchiku	50	medium	20 °C (68 °F)	medium	3–
Shippoden	55	weaker	20 °C (68 °F)	large	2–
Taiheiden	50	stronger	23 °C (73 °F)	large	2–
Tenzan	50	medium	20 °C (68 °F)	large	2–
Towaden	60	weaker	20 °C (68 °F)	medium	2–
SHUROCHIKU					
Kinsho	55	weaker	20 °C (68 °F)	medium	6–
Hakuseiden	65	weaker	20 °C (68 °F)	medium	6–
Shurochikuao	50	medium	18 °C (64 °F)	medium	3–

tics	From Average Quality Parents			From Choice Quality Parents		
eaf ckness	Percentage of Choice Shoots	Percentage of Average Shoots	Percentage of Poor Shoots	Percentage of Choice Shoots	Percentage of Average Shoots	Percentage of Poor Shoots
ı	100	...	...	100	...	...
ck	100	...	...	100	...	...
dium	100	...	...	100	...	...
ı	100	...	...	100	...	...
ı	100	...	...	100	...	...
ck	100	...	...	100	...	...
ı	100	...	...	100	...	...
ck	100	...	...	100	...	...
ı	100	...	...	100	...	...
ck	100	...	...	100	...	...
ck	100	...	...	100	...	...
dium	100	...	...	100	...	...
ı	100	...	...	100	...	...
ı	80	15	5	100	...	...
ı	25	25	60	40	35	25
ı	100	...	...	100	...	...

Every year, representatives of various local chapters of the Kansokai (Japan Kansochiku Association) gather to compile the kansochiku *meikan*, or directory. Based on each plant's beauty, price, and popularity, and considering that year's new varieties, the members rank the palms into four classes. Within each class, the most popular plants are given special recognition. These are starred in the translation below.

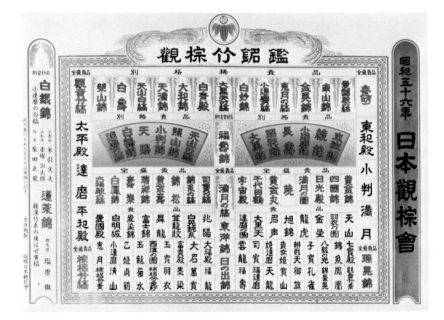

FIRST CLASS

Aikokudennoshima	Shirotaenishiki	Tenzanshiroshima
Nanzannishiki	Daikokutennoshima	Hakuju
Kinkonishiki	Hakuseiden	Eizannishiki
Keigetsunoshima	Yamatonishiki	Fukujunishiki*
Kodarumanoshima	Tenmanishiki	Mangetsunoshima*

SECOND CLASS

Tokainishiki	Showanishiki	Kobannishiki
Ayanishiki	Daikokunishiki	Tenshi
Kodarumanishiki	Tenzannoshima	Hakutsurunishiki
Choju	Shozannishiki	Darumanoshima

THIRD CLASS

Kotobuki*
Kannonchikushima*
Zuikonishiki*
Shurochikushima*
Toyonishiki*
Hinodenishiki*
Koganenishiki
Shikokunishiki

Nikkoden
Mangetsunozu
Akatsuki
Ogonmaru
Chiyodazuru
Uchuden
Shihonoshima

Kinshinoshima
Kinsho
Ogonju
Zuishonishiki
Juraku
Hakuhonishiki
Daifukudennoshima

FOURTH CLASS

Towaden*
Koban*
Mangetsu*
Taiheiden*
Daruma*
Heiwaden*
Tenzan
Hagoromonozu
Kimboshi
Ryuko
Asahinishiki
Meisei
Daikokuten
Darumanozu
Choyo
Hakkokinshi
Toryumon
Shoryu
Fujinishiki
Aizennishiki

Hakumeijo
Aikokuden
Shippoden
Kinshi
Hakkonohikari
Shiho
Benzaiten
Kijohime
Himedaruma
Shiho
Unryu
Daifukuden
Daimyo
Fukiden
Gyokuho
Seikainozu
Gyokuryu
Otohime
Kodaruma

Keigetsu
Kannonchikuao
Ho-o
Kinseiko
Kujaku
Mihata
Hozan
Tenryu
Fukudaruma
Fukuju
Fukuryu
Manpo
Sumizome
Hagoromo
Shurochikukinsha
Kikusui
Manazuru
Seizan
Shurochikuao

Glossary-Index

Numbers in italics indicate the page in Chapter 4 where the plant's general description appears.

137

application, 76, 100, 121, 128
  kinds, 98–100
flowers, 11
Fukiden, *38*
Fukuju, 21, 23, 24, 28, *38*, 114
Fukujunishiki, *22*
fungicides, 101, 108, 122

genealogy, 17–18
germination, 11
greenhouses, 66–94
  frame house, 86
  insulation, 87, 127
  plastic, 87
Gyokuho, *38*
Gyokuryu, *39*

Hagoromo, 35
Hagoromonozu, *35*
Hakkokinshi, 15, *23*, 30
Hakkonishiki, 26
Hakkonohikari, *23*
Hakuhonishiki, *23*
Hakuju, *24*, 38
Hakumeijo, *42*
Hakuseiden, *42*, 46
Hakutsurunishiki, *24*
heating, 90–93, 127
  charcoal, 92
  coal, 92
  electric, 93
  gas, 92
  kerosene, 92
height, 8
Heiwaden, 15, *39*, 40, 42
Himedaruma, *39*, 41
Hinodenishiki, 15, 19, *24*, 46
history, 13–16
Ho-o, 6, *39*
hormone, *see also* roots, 70
humidity, 94, 101, 125

imported group: plants from
  foreign countries other than
  Taiwan and China, 17
insects, 103–4, 108

scale, 103
insecticides, 104, 108, 122, 125,
  127–28

Kannon: Buddhist goddess of
  mercy, 6
kannonchiku: *Rhapis excelsa,* 3,
  6, 17, 19–42
Kannonchikushima, 15, 23, *25*,
  46
kansochiku: *Rhapis excelsa* and
  Rhapis humilis, 3
Kansokai: Japan Kansochiku As-
  sociation, 14, 46
Keigetsu, 15, *25*, 37, *39*
Keigetsunoshima, *25*
Kimboshi, 18, *43*
Kinkonishiki, 23, *26*
Kinkoraku, 29
Kinseiko, *35*
Kinshi, 15, 20, *26*, 34
Kinsho, 15, 18, *43*, 46
Koban, 15, 26, 37, *40*, 42, 114
Kobannishiki, *26*
Kodaruma, 27, 28, 34, 37, *40*, 114
Kodarumanishiki, *27*, 40
Kodarumanoshima, *27*
Koganenishiki, *27*, 40
Kotobuki, 15, 21, 23, 24, *28*, 38,
  46

landscaping, *see* outdoor cultivation
leaves, 8–10, 50–52, 54, 76, 84, 90,
  102, 108, 121
light, 76, 83, 85, 87, 89–90, 102,
  121, 127
location, 82–86, 121, 124–28

Mangetsu, 15, 29, 36, *40*
Mangetsunoshima, 22, *28*
Mangetsunozu, *36*
Meisei, *36*

Namikannonchiku, 24, *40*
Namishurochiku, *43*

Nanzannishiki, 22, *29*, 46
native group: plants introduced to Japan long ago, 17
Nikkoden, *29*

obtaining kansochiku, *see* sources
Ogonmaru, *29*
okihi: special fertilizer balls placed on soil surface, also called "place" fertilizer, 97–98, 100, 121, 126, 128
origin of kansochiku, 4, 6
Otohime, 39, *41*
outdoor cultivation, 105–10, 125, 127–28
    choice of variety, 105–6
    fertilizing, 108
    location, 106–8
    planting, 108
    soil, 108

"place" fertilizer, see *okihi*
planting, 74, 108
popularity, 14–15
pot size, 62–64, 70
pots, 60 62
potting mix, *see* soil
prices, 14, 15, 22, 45–46
propagation, *see also* commercial propagation, 5, 12, 65–76

quality (plant grades), 49–50

ranking table, 14
rejuvenating, *see also* air-layering, 70
Rhapis excelsa, 3, 6
Rhapis humilis, 3, 8
roots, 10–11, 62–63, 65, 70, 81, 98, 101–2

sana: cupped ceramic piece with seven holes to cover pot drain hole, 62, 74
sand, *see* soil
satsuki: azalea used for bonsai, 81

seasonal care, 124–28
seeds, 11
selecting kansochiku, 45–53, 118–20
separation, 66–76
    maintenance after, 76
    number of shoots to remove, 67
    root requirements, 67
    season, 65–66
shading, 85, 90
Shiho, 30, *41*
Shihonoshima, *30*, 41
shimafu: striped variegation, 3
Shippoden, 15, *41*
Shirotaenishiki, 23, *30*
Shoryu, *36*
Showanishiki, *30*
Shozannishiki, *31*
shurochiku: *Rhapis humilis*, 3, 6, 8, 17, 42–44
Shurochikuao, 42, *43*
Shurochikushima, 18, *43*, 46
soil, 56–58, 122
    nutrients, 58
    river sand, 56
sources of kansochiku, 46
sphagnum moss, 58, 70, 74, 81
spotted, *see* variegation
spring care, 124–25
stem (or trunk), 8
striped kansochiku, *see* variegation
summer care, 125–26

Taiheiden, 15, 39, 40, *41*
taiwanchiku group: plants originating in Taiwan, 17
temperature, 11, 66, 80, 82, 83, 86, 90, 93, 122, 125, 127–28
Tenmanishiki, *31*
Tenshi, *31*
Tenzan, 15, 30, 31, 32, 37, 40, *42*, 114
Tenzannoshima, 15, 21, 30, *32*, 33, 42
Tenzanshiroshima, 30, 31, *32*, 42, 46

Tokainishiki, 15, *32*, 46
Toryumon, 15, *36*
Towaden, *42*
Toyonishiki, *33*
transplanting, 77–81, 121
    season, 80

Uchuden, *33*

variegation
    origin, 13
    spotted, 3, 34
    stability, 46, 53
    stripe categories, 54
    striped, 3, 19–34
varieties
    number of, 16, 17, 45
    types, 19–44

ventilation, 86–87, 90, 124
water
    quality, 96
    rain, 96
    temperature, 96
    types, 96
watering, 76, 94–97, 122
winter care, 86–94, 108–9, 122, 127–28

Yamato Honzo: early botanical book, 6

zufu: spotted variegation, 3
Zuikonishiki, 15, 20, 24, 26, 33, *34,* 46, 69
Zuishonishiki, 27, *34,* 40

The "weathermark" identifies this book as a pro-
duction of John Weatherhill, Inc., publishers of fine
books on Asia and the Pacific. Book design and typography by Meredith
Weatherby and Ruth P. Stevens. Layout of illustrations by Yoshihiro
Murata. Composition, printing, and binding by Samhwa Printing
Company, Seoul. The typeface used is 11–point Monotype Baskerville.